COMBAT STRATEGY

Junsado: The Way of the Warrior

COMBAT STRATEGY

Junsado: The Way of the Warrior

by
Hanho

T   Turtle Press   Hartford

To contact the author or to order additional copies of this book write:

Turtle Press
PO Box 290206
Wethersfield, CT 06129-0206

Library of Congress Card Catalog Number 91-67891

ISBN 1-880336-01-4

Fifth Printing

Library of Congress Cataloging in Publication Data

Hanho, date
         Combat strategy: junsado, the way of the warrior / by Hanho.
                 p.   cm.
         Includes index.
         ISBN 1-880336-01-4
         1. Martial Arts. 2. Self-defense.   I. Title
    GV1101.H36   1992
    796.8--dc20   91-67891

戰師道

韓豪

NOTE TO READERS

Throughout this book, "he" is used to refer to people. This is for ease of reading only and should be taken to mean he or she where applicable.

BEFORE YOU BEGIN

Exercises and activities contained in this book are strenuous and may result in injury to the practitioner. As with all exercise programs, consult a physician before beginning. Skills contained in this book are dangerous and in some cases deadly and intended to be used only where lawfully and morally permissible. The reader assumes all responsibility for his use or misuse or information contained herein.

Contents

BOOK　　ONE

COMBAT　STRATEGY

CHAPTER 1

COMBAT

Conflict between opposing forces. This is the most universal definition of combat. The concept of combat is that of opposition, resistance, competition, discord. And in many instances, this is the reality. Most conflict is born of animosity, anger, fear, hate or another negative emotion.

But there is another type of combat, that of warriors, those trained in the art of combat, not just the skills. They may begin the fight out of emotion, but once they engage the opponent, emotion disappears. It is replaced by total concentration and dedication to a single ideal - victory.

At its highest levels, combat is comprised of two forces moving not against each other, but in harmony with each other. They are not compelled by emotions or fears. They are in full control of their actions and understand the actions of their opponent. Like a physical game of chess, they plan many moves in advance and estimate their opponent's actions and reactions based on training, experience and intuition. This combat is beyond the combat of conflict.

But what is the difference between beating the opponent with an emotional attack or beating him with a well composed mind? The results are the same. Each method will make the fighter victorious if he has the physical skills to apply. But what if he doesn't? What if he faces a highly skilled or physically superior opponent? Anger alone will not carry him to victory.

When the opponent is superior in any way, the untrained fighter will have great difficulty in defeating him. The skilled fighter will have a dramatic advantage, allowing him to overcome his disadvantages and turn them into advantages. He will coordinate his skills to attack the most vulnerable parts of the opponent and defeat him with a minimum of effort.

This is where combat becomes harmony within conflict. Harmony inside oneself and harmony with one's surroundings. The skilled fighter trains not to oppose his opponent, but to flow with him. This does not mean that he is passive. He has a set strategy for fighting, but he is not confined by it. If he finds a better way, he can adapt any time. He does not resist the rhythm and flow of the fight itself.

The skill of harmonizing in combat is one that is acquired through practice and experience. It does not come from practice alone. Practice can prepare you, but only experiencing the reality of engaging another person in physical conflict can lead you to understand the intricacies of combat.

COMBAT RHYTHM

Combat is a series of visible and concealed maneuvers whose goal is to destroy the opponent and bring victory. The visible maneuvers include planning, practice and the physical actions you take to attack the opponent and defend yourself during combat. The concealed maneuvers are the psychological preparation and the covert strategies and tactics you employ in the fight.

A combination of both concealed and visible maneuvers is necessary to defeat an opponent. If you are physically very strong and well conditioned, but uninformed regarding fighting strategy, you will defeat unskilled opponents easily through brute force, but you will be outwitted by skilled tacticians. Conversely, if you have a brilliant tactical mind, but spend little time for perfecting your physical weapons, you will have trouble implementing your brilliant strategy.

In both cases, unbalanced training leads to defeat. To be successful, combine the tools of combat skills and physical training with a blue print of well-planned and adaptable strategy. Imagine having a blueprint for a beautiful house and not having any tools or lumber with which to build it. All you have is a drawing. It has no practical function unless you act on it. Or what about having many tools and materials without knowing where to begin building. The chances of ending up with a dream house are small.

The same is true for combat skills and strategy. Know where you are going, how you will get there and what tools you will need along the way.

There is one additional necessity - adaptation. The ability to adapt your tools or plans according to how the current situation is changing is essential . Suppose you have your blueprint and the required tools and materials for your house. You begin to dig a hole for the basement and find that the ground is solid rock. If you stick to your original plan, you will expend a large amount of energy to create very little gain. Here, it is wise to revise your original plan according to your newly gathered facts.

The human element of combat creates many instances of change. What appeared to be possible becomes impossible. What appeared to be unrealistic, becomes realistic. Constantly monitor the current circumstances to see if you can adapt your strategy or tactics to a better course of action. Watch for unexpected openings and be prepared with alternative plans when your original fails.

There is no absolute formula for victory in combat. There are conventional and unconventional strategies that have been tested and used for thousands of years, but none of them is fail-safe. Conventional strategies are the most proven, but they are also the best known. They are susceptible to counter tactics by skilled opponents.

But you must understand the conventional strategies to prepare for combat. Begin from the conventional and adapt it to your own character and skills to create a unique style that is suitable for you. This is not to say that you should totally dispose of the conventional tactics and strategies of combat. They are very valuable and will make up the foundation of your training.

They are not, however, the sole means by which victory may be achieved. There are endless variations on the conventional skills that can be created and used in unique ways by individual fighters according to their own personal strengths and weaknesses. Every individual is unique and should look for the advantages their uniqueness presents.

TYPES OF COMBAT

There are several categories of combat among humans. Combat can be arranged such as boxing, wrestling, or martial arts practice. It also can be spontaneous, as in fighting and self-protection. The difference lies in the imposition or lack of rules and the level of conflict between the contestants.

Arranged combat is a common way of testing combat skills. It can be among friends or rivals. It can be for fun or high-stakes. It can be with strict safety rules or anything goes type matches. Most often, however, it is contested with the safety of the contestants in mind and the outcome is secondary.

Arranged combat is a good method of practicing skills within a framework of safety rules. For maximum results, it should allow the widest range of attacks and defenses possible. If you train for the possibility of a life-endangering encounter, you should not be limited by unnecessary rules and gear that will not exist in the anticipated attack.

For example, a woman who trains for self-protection would not gain much by putting on boxing gloves and sparring according to boxer's rules. She is unlikely to face an attacker who will give the room to punch and she runs the risk of seriously damaging her hands in a bare-handed attack. A more realistic approach for her would be to engage in simulation training in which she is faced with an attempted assault and practices thwarting the attacker.

Arranged combat should closely model its goals. If its goal is sport, train for sport. If its goal is self-protection, train for realism with a minimum of rules and a heavy dose of reality.

When spontaneous combat does occur, you will need to be prepared mentally and physically. Spontaneous combat can arise from a dispute with an acquaintance or a physical attack by a stranger. It can happen anytime, to anyone.

There are two levels of spontaneous combat: psychological and physical. The former often leads to the latter. To prepare for the mental and physical realities of combat, practice maintaining a calm mind during training. Every human conflict arises from emotion. Controlling your emotion is the key to controlling the course of the conflict. If you become controlled by your emotions, you have a greater chance to make errors in judgment that will lead to your defeat.

To prepare for spontaneous combat, design a training program that blends your mental and physical strengths. Combine psychological and physical tactics to defeat the opponent on both levels. In fact, if an opponent is psychologically over matched, he may back down out of fear. Being well prepared will enhance your capability to assess the circumstances and implement a workable strategy to establish your advantage.

FACTORS AFFECTING COMBAT

The outcome of any physical confrontation is determined by several interconnected factors. The most important and controllable factors are those qualities that make up **your combat skills**:

1. Ability
2. Instinct
3. Strategy
4. Determination
5. Physical condition
6. Efficiency
7. Adaptability
8. Experience

Each of these elements can be cultivated through consistent and effective training. Examine them in more detail to see how they affect the outcome of the confrontation:

ABILITY

Your physical ability is determined by the amount and quality of your practice. Every practice session should have a specific goal and every movement should be practiced with its application in mind. Avoid random or aimlessly repetitious practice.

INSTINCT

Instinct is an intangible quality that gives you the edge in decision making and planning. Instinct is the sum of information collected by your senses that is not readily obvious to your conscious mind. It often produces a ''feeling'' that something is wrong or right without a logical explanation. When you are uncertain what to do next or how to handle an opponent, rely on your gut feelings. The more experience you have in combat, the more reliable your instincts will be.

STRATEGY

Strategy is the map you follow through combat. It begins when you first see your opponent and ends when the opponent is subdued. Strategy is like a game plan or a play book from which you select your course of action according to the opponent and situation presented. Strategy will be covered in great depth in later chapters.

DETERMINATION

Determination and stamina play a large role in combat where the fighters are equally matched. When physical skills are similar, the winner will be decided by sheer guts and determination. Whoever is able to fight harder and resist longer will be the victor. To build mental and physical stamina, train through feelings of fatigue and mild discomfort, and engage regularly in contact sparring/training.

PHYSICAL CONDITION

Like skill development, conditioning requires regular, focused practice. Set a workout schedule that is suitable for your training goals. Include exercises for endurance, timing, strength, speed and reflexes in your regular workouts. Set regular long and short term fitness goals for motivation and to track your progress.

EFFICIENCY

Being efficient is important in any physical activity. Your body has a limited supply of energy to burn at any given time. Conserving energy is of the utmost importance to enable you to engage in prolonged or strenuous physical activity. If both you and your opponent have a similar amount of energy to expend during a bout, the one who uses it more efficiently will be the one who delivers the final blow.

ADAPTABILITY

Being able to adapt to the flow of the confrontation is essential. Adaptation means assessing your needs and selecting the correct and necessary actions for fulfilling them. Without adaptation, you may become the victim of your own strategy. Strategy is very transparent and a skillful fighter can quickly assess and counter his opponent. Emphasize variety in your training and experiment with variations of your favorite techniques to avoid becoming stale.

EXPERIENCE

There is only one way to gain experience and that is to repeatedly engage in your target activity . If this is not possible, engage in the most realistic simulations possible. Experience a variety of opponent types and styles to test the validity of your skills and discover new approaches. The more experienced you are, the more insightful you can be in developing a successful strategy.

Development of these eight elements directly and dramatically affects your fighting skills. Before you can win over your opponent, you have to master your own body and mind. Go into combat knowing you are fully prepared and in top condition. When you confidently approach your opponent, your chances of defeating him are greater.

Once you have fully prepared yourself, you can begin to analyze the other factors that affect combat:

1. Your opponent's qualities
2. Terrain
3. Environment
4. Weapons

The same qualities that you develop in yourself are important to **your opponent** as well. When you face an opponent ask yourself these questions:

1. Ability

What is his level of physical ability? How much has he trained? What are his favorite skills? How does his skill level compare to mine?

2. Instinct

Is he prepared with many set formulas/combinations or does he go with the flow of the fight? Is he able to make quick decisions when confused or surprised? Are his movements loose and fluid, without hesitation?

3. Strategy

What style fighter is he: in-fighter/out-fighter, tall/short, strength/speed, left handed/right handed/ambidextrous, aggressive/defensive, etc.? Is an initiative attacker or a counterattacker? Does he use conventional tactics or unconventional skills? What are his primary and secondary vital openings?

4. Determination

Is he psychologically determined to win? Is he focused or distracted? Does he tire quickly or is he able to respond to your strongest attacks with equal strength?

5. Physical Condition

What is his physical condition like? Does he appear fit, strong, quick, agile? What are his strong and weak areas of conditioning? How can I exploit his weaknesses?

6. Efficiency

Is he making many unnecessary movements? Does he conserve energy by flowing with you or does he expend energy for resisting? Are his movements focused or underdeveloped?

7. Adaptability

Can he easily adapt to your changes in tactics and strategy? Is he locked into one style? Is he vulnerable to counter attacks because his style is one dimensional? Is he psychologically sensitive to your changes in tactics?

8. Experience

How experienced is he? How does he approach me, is he calm or nervous? Is he checking on me or busy with himself?

You may or may not be able to answer all or even any of these questions, but they will give you some guidelines for assessing your opponents. After studying this book and practicing with a variety of opponents, the ability to analyze opponents with a minimum of conscious thought will develop.

Once you have determined the type of opponent you are facing, consider the type of **terrain** on which you will fight. You may be indoors or out, on a hill or a plain, on stairs or in a confined area, on slippery or wet ground, etc. Each type of terrain requires special consideration. Some will give you an advantage, some will cause you difficulty. Train in an assortment of places to improve your adaptability to varying terrain.

Similar to terrain is **environment**. The combat environment may be confining or treacherous. Fighting can occur any time, anywhere. Training in a cushioned, well-lighted, spacious area will not prepare for fighting in the dark, the rain, a closet, a car, a stairwell, a steep hill, a river or an icy street. Use environmental simulations to prepare both psychologically and physically for disadvantageous environments.

The final factor to prepare for is the availability of **weapons** to you and your opponent. One or both of you may enter the fight with a weapon, or there may be environmental weapons available to whomever is wise enough to use them. If one of you has a weapon at the start of the fight, adapt your strategy accordingly. If you see something around you, a heavy or sharp object that you can use to gain an edge over your opponent, grab it and use it before your opponent gets the same idea.

Do not depend on a weapon for your strategy. Use a weapon as an enhancement for your plan. Every weapon can be lost during the fight or can be taken and used by your opponent. Therefore, it is important to know not only how to use your weapon, but how to defend against and neutralize it as well.

THE ULTIMATE COMBAT

The ultimate combat situation is one in which you are able to finish your opponent with one initiative attack. This does not necessarily mean a single blow. It means finishing the fight with the strategy and tactics you planned without interference from your adversary.

Not everyone is able to finish with a single blow, due to size and strength disadvantages. But regardless of your size or strength, you can win in one initiative if you plan and carry out a perfect strategy. This is the essence of Junsado. Assess the situation, plan what will work for you and implement it perfectly. If your assessment is accurate, your plan fitting for both you and your opponent, and your implementation flawless, you will experience the ultimate in combat.

CHAPTER 2
STRATEGY

Strategy is a plan or method for maximum utilization of power through long range planning and development to obtain a specific goal, such as to ensure security or victory. Strategy begins long before the confrontation. It begins with your first day of training. If you train well, with a goal in mind, your strategy is already being carried out.

By seeing training as a part of your overall combat strategy, you conserve time and energy. You will be well conditioned to perform the movements required to implement your strategy. You also will have confidence in adapting your training to actual combat, because your training has been modeled after real combat all along.

Strategy is long range and intricate. It takes careful consideration and purposeful thinking. Strategy allows you to maximize what you already have through skillful execution of your best weapons. Strategy should not be confused, however, with tactics. Tactics are the actual deployment of the physical skills you have prepared. Strategy is the map and tactics are the vehicle you use to navigate the course you have plotted. One without the other is like being lost without a map or having a map without viable transportation - useless.

STRATEGY AS DECEPTION

Strategy is essentially deception. It is a means of winning through planning and analysis. Your opponent will not allow you to win. So strategy draws the situation into your favor by deceiving your opponent into thinking he can win where he cannot. You give him an apparently favorable situation, when, in fact, you have set a trap to defeat him.

Deception has many aspects. It can be small scale or large scale. It can be obvious or unseen. Sometimes the most obvious deception is the best. Imagine an opponent who rushes into the fight without any apparent plan or apprehension. He appears to be nothing but a wild bull on a rampage. Immediately you will think, what a fool. I can effortlessly defeat him. He has no skill or strategy. I can outsmart him easily.

But maybe you have already fallen victim to his strategy. Perhaps making you think he has no strategy is his strategy. While you plot how to defeat him, he will overwhelm and immobilize you. His strategy is to make you overconfident and overly analytic. While you are thinking, he is fighting.

This is the ultimate strategy; one that is not apparent until the fight is over.

To deceive the opponent, simply pretend something that is not true. Become an actor on a stage. The better you act, the easier it will be to implement your strategy. Deceive your opponent into being busy. The busier he is reacting to your deception, the less time he will have to think about attacking you.

Create many feints, fakes and draws that are convincing. Sometimes fake and sometimes attack. Make your opponent wonder at your every movement, it is a real attack or a fake? Keep his mind busy and insecure. Cause him to make useless movements and disrupt his plans. Take advantage of his mistakes. Cause him to miss. Make him defend against your fake attacks. Make him expend large amounts of energy without getting positive results.

Never let him become confident or comfortable with your style. Defeat him psychologically and you are half way to victory.

STRATEGIC PLANNING

In fishing, baiting a hook and reeling in an unsuspecting fish is preferable to chasing the fish around the ocean until you catch him. Unless you can swim better than the fish, you better stay in your boat and make him come to you. Strategy is the same. Why chase after your opponent and run into his territory if you can make him come to you?

Set traps that will lure your opponent into your psychological and physical territory. Give him an irresistible opportunity (the bait) and prepare a stunning counter attack (the hook) when he takes your bait. When setting a trap, take care not to expose it too soon. If you show your trap before he has fully committed, he will withdraw and he will not return for another bait soon.

Conversely, do not wait too long. If he bites and gets stung by your trap, he will be furious. If you do not stun him into inaction, he will redouble his resolve to beat you. Waiting too long will result in a ferocious counter by your opponent.

Timing is of the essence for baiting the opponent. Maintain your composure and let the opponent rush into you. While he is busy moving, mentally step back and with full alertness, view him like a fish circling your hook.

Stay detached and wait for the perfect moment to hook him and attack. Maintain a relaxed, ready posture and mind. Pick your chance and finish him when you are at a strategic advantage.

DIRECT LINE OF ATTACK

In combat, planning to attack along the most direct and economical line is key. Be quick and concise without hesitation.   However, do not mistake the most direct route for the shortest physical distance between your weapon and the target. The shortest route to accomplishing your goal may appear circuitous to the eye. But once put into action, it will be the most effective.

Imagine yourself traveling in a boat, charting a straight course to your destination. Unexpectedly, lying directly ahead of you in your path is an island. If you want to reach your destination, you have to make a decision. You can go around the island by way of the boat or you can sail up to island, carry your boat across the island and then get back in the boat and sail on your way.

Crossing on land is the shortest distance from one side of the island to the other. It is not, however, the most efficient. The most efficient route is to sail around the island. Although this appears to be a digressive route in terms of distance, it is the more pragmatic in terms of energy expended. A boat is not meant to be carried over land, it is meant to travel in water.

Carrying a boat over land just to take the shortest route from Point A to Point B ignores the purpose of the boat. When traveling by boat, make the most efficient possible use of the boat. Though it does not readily appear to be the shortest way, it has other advantages.

Be flexible. If your original plan of traveling straight ahead is not feasible by boat, you must adapt your course to what you currently have available.

Combat is the same. Travel the route of least resistance with the tools you have. Don't be attached to appearances or plans. Sometimes the obviously direct route will be best and sometimes the less obvious direct route will be best. The best direct route is the one that maximizes the function of the techniques being used.

STRATEGY OF OFFENSE AND DEFENSE

To formulate your strategy properly, study the function of offense and defense. Offense is the art of attacking the opponent's weaknesses. Defense is the art of using your strongest weapons to form an impenetrable shield around your body, especially your weak points.

There are several types of defense. The best defense is one that does not give the opponent the opportunity to attack, thereby avoiding any chance of being hit. The second best defense is one that can cut, evade or block any attack the opponent launches while incurring little or no damage.

The first case is the ideal goal of your training. In the best type of defense, defense and offense become one. There is no thought about which movements are defensive and which are offensive. Every movement is so well executed that the opponent has no chance to launch an effective attack. You give him neither a vulnerable target nor a chance to attack.

Defensive movement   Offensive movement

Offense and defense in one movement

This is an underlying principle of Junsado. Every movement is executed to attack directly without providing opportunities to the opponent. For example, imagine an assailant attempts to punch you in the face. The conventional strategy of offense and defense dictates that you first block his punch and then counter attack. While blocking, you momentarily leave yourself vulnerable to attack.

The strategy of offense and defense as one, dictates that you move inside his punching range and launch a series of attacks before he is able to strike you. In this type of strategy, there is no offense or defense. There is only one movement that accomplishes your goal of ending the fight and maintaining your safety. Keep this goal in mind when you plan and execute your best skills.

Strategy goes forward regardless of what the opponent attempts, yet at the same time, is sensitive to the changes of the confrontation. To execute properly, you must know when to stick to your plan and when to change course. This means not being deceived by your opponent's strategy. Know what is real and what is illusion created by your opponent to trick you.

When you cannot make the ideal movement that combines offense and defense, fall back on a combination of offensive skills and defensive skills. Defense is for protecting yourself when you are not prepared or strong enough to launch an effective attack. It is based on making your strategy, tactics and physical/psychological condition strong enough to resist attack. It depends on your strength and preparation.

Offense is primarily those actions that deploy your superior strengths and whose goal is to defeat the opponent. It is reliant partly on you and partly on your opponent. To defeat the opponent, your offense must be more than just good in the conventional sense. It also must be superior to your opponent's defense. If you prepare excellent kicks and your opponent is better at blocking your kicks than you are at deploying them, you will lose.

Here it would be better to have another type of offense to fall back on. In this sense, superior does not always mean technically better. It can mean smarter, faster, stronger, more sophisticated. The offense that wins is the one that best fits your strengths and your opponent's weaknesses.

In summary, when you master offense, the opponent will not know how to defend against you. When you master defense, he will have nowhere to attack. If you master the strategy of offense and defense as one, he will not even know whether to attack or defend.

CHAPTER 3
JUNSADO AS
COMBAT STRATEGY

The natural phenomena of the universe are ever changing. Combat is not an exception. Junsado techniques are grounded in the principles of change. Changes in you, changes in your opponent, changes in the environment are all considered in Junsado strategy. It is a living art.

Junsado skills are applicable across a wide range of situations and styles. They are meant to evolve and adapt to the individual fighter. They are the system of no system that is necessary to meet the challenges of combat.

In combat, preformed concepts are not enough to meet the demands of the anything-goes reality of fighting. Don't be confined by styles, rules, forms, favoritism or even common sense. Thinking only one way is apt to lead you into a trap. This way, that way, low way, high way, straight way, round way, slow hit, fast hit. There are so many ways to choose from. No way includes every way. That is what junsado stands for - free thinking, no limitations, freedom.

This is not to say that you should throw all convention out and train randomly. The ability to think freely comes from understanding the basic conventional concepts that lie within a system. For example, without knowing the numerical system, how can you learn how to add and subtract, multiply and divide? And without learning basic numerical functions, how can you perform simple daily functions like calculating your change in a store?

When you learn to add, you practice by adding specific equations under the guidance of a teacher. Through this tutelage, you learn the principles of addition. There is no way for you to practice and memorize every numerical equation you will ever need in life. Once you master the principles of addition, you can add whatever sum is presented to you without difficulty.

The addition you practice is not the end product of your learning, it is merely one step on your way to mathematical competency. However, the rules of adding remain constant in every country throughout the world. Everyone adds different equations, but all use the same rules.

In combat, you begin from learning how to make basic physical movements of attack and defense, similar to learning how to count. You then learn how to combine these movements in arranged applications, like learning the rules of addition. Once proficient in applications, you can apply your skills to many situations according to the specific demands, like adding your pocket change or determining how much your grocery bill will be.

Each step requires following the system until you learn and master its principles. Once you master the principles, you are free to apply them in many ways.

Addition and subtraction each have their own important function. We cannot say addition is better than subtraction or vice versa. Each is important in its own merit. Therefore, junsado incorporates many types of skills. Sometimes you will need kicking and punching, sometimes grappling, sometimes a combination of both.

Neither is any better or worse than the other. It is a matter of appropriateness. Add when you must add. Subtract when you must subtract. Kick when you must kick. Throw when you must throw. Through the system of junsado, you will come to understand the appropriateness of each skill, so you can adapt a strategy and fighting style that is most fitting for you.

JUNSADO PRINCIPLES

Junsado principles are divided into two elements: tactics and strategy. Junsado tactics are a balanced combination of power and deception. Power is created by taking advantage of the most direct line of force and pinpointing the most vulnerable targets. Deception is caused by using a variety of skills and approaches to the opponent.

Junsado strategy is composed of primary and secondary responses. A primary response is a way of neutralizing the opponent's attack through one of four possible types of actions: 1) evasion (emptying the space), 2) parrying (redirecting the line of attack), 3) blocking (obstructing the line of attack) or 4) cutting (filling the space). A primary response is usually followed by a secondary response.

The goal of the secondary response is to end the confrontation as efficiently as possible. The secondary response includes hand skills, elbow strikes, knee techniques, foot skills, takedowns, throws and joint immobilizations. The key to effective use of primary and secondary response skills is in the ability to select appropriate techniques according to the situation and opponent. This ability comes from practice and experience.

TRAINING

As any fighter knows, excellent physical conditioning is prerequisite to learning combat skills. Physical and mental strength are an essential foundation on which to build your fighting skills. To increase your fundamental physical condition, practice healthy habits in your everyday life. Adopt a daily conditioning and exercise program that exercises the whole body and especially the muscles and joints used in your combat training. The conditioning routine on Tape One in the Junsado Video Training Series is an excellent way to prepare.

Based on your physical conditioning, start practicing the basic fighting sills presented in Book Two: Fundamentals. If you are not currently actively participating in an exercise program, it is highly recommended that you have your exercises capabilities assessed by a qualified professional before proceeding.

When you are ready to begin, take the skills one at a time or in small groups and work slowly at first. Because the basic skills of combat are dynamic movements, it is highly recommended that you learn them from a qualified instructor or from Tape One in the Junsado Video Training Series. Each skill is a dynamic entity that cannot be expressed except through movement. The Fundamentals section of this book is intended as companion guide to personal or video instruction.

When you begin a new skill or movement, first visualize the ideal action. See yourself performing accurate, fluid movements. Begin practicing slowly, with the focus on imitating the correct line of movement. Refine each skill individually adding speed and power when you have established the correct movement pattern.

Once you have practiced a technique thoroughly, begin practice with a partner. Start with arranged interactions and limited skills. Increase the spontaneity of the interaction as your skills develop. Always use excellent control when practicing with a partner. These skills are meant for self-protection in actual combat and may cause serious injury if control is not exercised.

Throughout this book and the Junsado Video Training Series, there are many examples of effective combinations and techniques. They are intended to show you the possibilities of each skill. They are only some of the skills that you might need. See them as a guide to developing your own arsenal of effective skills.

When you look at a sample technique or combination, analyze it carefully. First look at the primary response. What is it? Why is it effective? How will it work best for you?

Consider the secondary responses that follow. How are they combined? Which targets are they intended for? How can you adapt them to fit your body type and ability?

Through the sample combinations, you will find several principles that run through junsado. The backfist, hook kick and knee strike are the main striking weapons. Joint immobilizations are used frequently to finish attackers, especially when the defendant is highly disadvantaged. Every skill has a unique purpose in training and execution.

As you practice each skill, you will come to understand its applications and purpose. Then you are ready to adapt it to fit your own physical and psychological style. Adaptation is the foundation of effectiveness in junsado. When you master and adapt junsado skills, they will fit you perfectly. They will become part of you.

USING THIS BOOK

In Book One, we have covered the general principles of combat strategy and a brief overview of junsado. In your daily life, pay careful attention to the phenomenon of change that is constantly taking place around you. In this change, there are underlying principles of combat. This is what Book One is about.

Book Two covers the fundamental tools of junsado. Book Three teaches you how to use the tools through proper strategy and tactics. Book Two and Three together form the core of junsado science.

Book Four is the art of junsado. It teaches you how to go beyond conventional tactics.

Book Five is the final stage of junsado. The ultimate goal of a warrior is to find harmony within oneself, with the universe, with humanity and with life itself.

BOOK TWO

FUNDAMENTALS

INTRODUCTION

Fundamentals are the tools you use to execute the strategy and tactics of junsado. They are common to many fighting disciplines around the world because they are the most useful and practical unarmed fighting skills developed by man.

In this section each fundamental skill is briefly described and illustrated to familiarize you with its basic concept. This section is not intended to teach you how to perform the movements. For learning the individual skills, there is no substitute for personal instruction or instructional videos. Every movement is a living entity and must be studied in action, not in words.

Study the theories found here and apply them to your physical training to develop skills with increased depth. Look for some aspect of the movement that was previously unknown or unclear to you.

When practicing fundamental skills, strive for perfection in every step of the movement. Break down the movement into its most basic components and practice each stage with careful attention to detail. Every movement has five stages:

1. **Preparation** is the actions you take to ready yourself for the movement.
2. **Execution** is the initiation and path of the movement as it advances to the target.
3. **Impact** is the culmination of the execution when you deliver the total force created by your weight and momentum to the target.
4. **Follow through** is the actions that follow the impact to complete the path of the movement
5. **Finish** is the relaxed and natural withdrawal of the body part used in the movement.

Practice each skill in the fundamentals section according to these stages to develop insight into the essence of the movement.

CHAPTER 1
STANCE

The stance is the foundation from which every technique is launched. It creates the firm ground for strong attacks and the agility for speedy attacks. It is not, however, a fixed foundation.

In free combat, the stances of the combatants are in constant flux. To identify a specific stance in the flurry of action is almost impossible. There appears to be a ceaseless combination of transitional movements as the fighters struggle for the advantage.

Junsado training recognizes both the need for transition and the need for a strong foundation by categorizing stances by type rather than fixed positions. At the most basic level there are two types of stance: half stance and full stance.

A full stance is one that is characterized by a reserved defensive posture. It allows for speed and transition with little commitment. Half stance, its complement, is any stance characterized by a strong, offensive, forward oriented posture. It builds a secure base for close fighting and grappling skills.

In this section, we will begin with the most basic versions of half and full stance. From these models you will find many variations that are necessary in combat. Stance is the basis for movement. Every stance should enhance the movement that is build upon it.

FULL STANCE

The full stance is principally a defensive stance used in the primary response. It allows you to maintain a safe distance from an aggressor and to cover your most vulnerable targets. It also permits easy forward and backward body movement for quickly retreating and advancing in the opening moments of a confrontation.

Full stance is important defensively. If you assume a committed stance too early in the fight, your opponent can set you up for an easy counterattack. Full stance should be used throughout the primary attack and in the early stages of the secondary attack to "feel out" the direction of the encounter and remain flexible until an opening appears.

The full stance maximizes the use of the front arm and leg for blocking and the rear arm and leg for countering movements. It also is ideal for quick transitional moves like grabbing, cutting and lightning strikes to the face and lower body. By combining quick frontal movement with easy body shifting, full stance allows you to close the distance abruptly and move to your secondary response.

The position of your hips also makes it easy to perform back leg kicks and spinning movements as counterattacks. In full stance, your rear foot is at a one hundred eighty degree angle to your front foot. From this position, you can turn your upper body to the rear and shoot your rear leg out on a straight line to initiate the spinning techniques.

In a defensive full stance, the weight of the body is neutral (equally balanced on both feet), whereas in an offensive posture the weight is shifted to the front foot.

All of the movements made from full stance have a clear advantage. They allow you to strike quickly and economically while protecting the vital points along the center line of your body.

Advantages of Full Stance

1. Front arm and leg prepared for quick defense
2. Vital targets along center line are covered
3. Easy attack and counter by front arm or leg without risk of exposing vulnerable targets
4. Easy forward/backward mobility to feel out the opponent in early stages of combat
5. Front arm and leg positioned for quick transitional and initiating movements
6. Long range stance to preserve safety zone

Techniques that Work Best with Full Stance

Defensive	Offensive
Front arm block	Front hand back fist
Front leg cut block	Front leg stomp kick
Rear hand direct counter	Rear leg hook kick
Rear leg direct counter	Rear leg back kick
Rear hand spin counter	Front leg cross leg throw
Rear leg spin counter	

Full Stance
front view

Full Stance
side view

How to Make Full Stance Correctly

1. Place both feet on one line aiming at the opponent.
2. Bend your knees slightly.
3. Relax your shoulders and turn slightly forward - expose 20-30 % of your body and conceal 70-80%.
4. Bend your arms ninety degrees at the elbows and raise your hands to shoulder height or relax your arms naturally at your sides.
5. Your fists may be opened or clenched.
6. Look into your opponent.

HALF STANCE

Half stance is an offensive, aggressive stance used primarily in close fighting circumstances. Once you come in contact with your opponent, switch to half stance and commit to your secondary response. By creating a stable base and freeing your upper and lower body for easy lateral movement, half stance allows you to attack strongly and confidently with a wide variety of striking and grappling skills.

Half stance is recommended for grappling, locking, throwing, joint immobilization, choking and grabbing. It also allows for great variety in lateral attacks using both right and left limbs without the need for pivoting or turning. Use full stance to overpower and confuse your opponent.

Defensively it is effective in resistance and lateral evasion in both close and neutral ranges. Avoid using half stance during medium range combat and in transitional movements when it is difficult to block incoming attacks. Half stance is vulnerable defensively because you are facing your opponent head on and exposing many prime targets.

Advantages of Half Stance

1. Stable base for engaging opponent
2. Good lateral movement
3. Allows random attacks from both sides
4. Strong stance for grappling and close fighting

Techniques that Work Best with Half Stance

Defensive	Offensive
Resisting	Cut-in
Lateral evasion	Throwing
Opening blocks	Locking
Downward blocks	Choking
Pulling/Pushing	Knee attack
	Punching
	Elbow strike

Half Stance
front view

Half Stance
side view

How to Make Half Stance Correctly

1. Position your back foot at a forty-five degree angle to your front foot.
2. Turn your hips and upper body forward.
3. Bend your knees slightly forward.
4. Bend your elbows ninety degrees and raise your hands to shoulder height.
5. Place your hands approximately shoulder distance apart and open or close them as you feel comfortable.

CHAPTER 2
FOOTWORK

The illustrations in this chapter represent the fundamental types of footwork necessary for combat. The footwork is broken down into half stance and full stance to demonstrate the types of movements best for each type of stance.

The darkened circles portray the original foot position and the open circles portray the finishing foot position. Some steps are marked with ones (1) to indicate the foot that will move first. In the case of a pivot, the open circle is placed over the darkened circle with only the direction of the foot changing.

The footwork illustrated here is shown throughout the junsado instructional series. Practice it thoroughly so you will be prepared to use it spontaneously.

FULL STANCE FOOTWORK

DEFENSIVE		
	Right stance	Left Stance
1. Back slide		
2. Lateral slide		
3. Back step (left, right)		
4. Lateral step (left, right) 30 to 45 degree angle		

OFFENSIVE		
	Right stance	Left stance
1. Forward slide		
2. Lateral forward slide 30 to 45 degree angle		
3. Forward step		
4. Lateral forward step 30 to 45 degree angle		

HALF STANCE FOOTWORK

	OFFENSIVE	
	Right stance	Left stance
1. Forward slide		
2. Lateral forward slide		
3. Forward step		
4. Lateral forward step		

CHAPTER 3
HAND   SKILLS

Hand skills are used most frequently in self-protection because the human hands have highly developed capabilities. With the capacity to grab, the hand is superior to any other self-protection mechanism. Without the ability to grasp the opponent, throwing, choking and locking skills would be virtually impossible.

The hands provide the quickest, shortest route to the opponent's vital areas, especially those on the head. Hand attacks are used in short and medium range combat.   Obviously, the opponent should be no farther than slightly beyond arm's length when you launch a hand attack. Practice speed and deception in hand skills.

In addition to offense, the hand provides a natural defense due to its position at the end of the arm. If you drop or raise your arms naturally, you will find that they easily extend to cover all your vital points including your groin, internal organs, throat and head. Easy mobility, maneuverability and natural proportions make the hands and arms unique weapons.

CLOSED HAND STRIKES

STRAIGHT PUNCH

Key: The straight punch provides the most direct route of attack for the fist to the high and middle section targets.

Targets: Frontal face, solar plexus

HOOK PUNCH

Key: The hook moves in an inward arc that utilizes the angle of the elbow to unify the force of the upper body and the fist.

Targets: Torso, jaw

UPPERCUT

Key: The uppercut moves in an upward arc using the angle of the elbow to unify the power of the hips and lower body with the impact force of the fist.

Targets: Chin, groin, diaphragm,

DOWNWARD PUNCH

Key: The downward punch moves in the opposite direction of the uppercut and is based on the same concept of force through unification.

Targets: Face, sternum

BACKFIST

Key:
Straight - directly to the target
Circular - with a wide follow through
Downward - a downward arc to the target
Spinning - with a three quarter turn to the rear

Targets:
Straight - Jaw, frontal face
Circular - Jaw, ear, neck
Downward - Jaw, face
Spinning - Ear, jaw

HAMMERFIST

Key:
Inside - striking with the palm facing upwards
Reverse - striking with the palm facing downward
Downward - striking with the palm facing laterally
Backward - against an attack from the rear

Targets: Jaw, ribs, face, kidneys, groin, thigh, spine

OPEN HAND STRIKES

FINGER JAB

Key: The front hand finger jab uses a quick snapping movement to stun, distract or set-up the opponent. The rear hand finger jab uses a power strike to cause severe pain to soft vital targets.

Targets: Eyes, nose, throat

KNIFE STRIKE

Key: The knife strike makes maximum usage of the snapping force created by the shoulder and elbow. It has three variations: inside, reverse and downward.

Targets: Neck, frontal face, temple, rib cage, biceps, elbow, rear knee

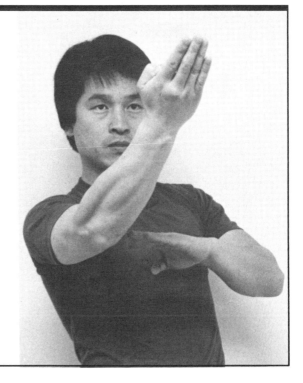

BACK HAND

Key: The back hand creates a whipping motion to confuse and emotionally defeat the opponent. Use it for a strong psychological impact before the main technique.

Targets: Face, ear

PALM PUSH

Key: Palm pushing is done in a straight or angular direction to apply pressing force to move the opponent.

Targets: Jaw, chin, nose, chest, ribs, kidneys

PALM STRIKE

Key: Palm striking is a linear strike used to create impact with the heel of the palm.

Targets: Jaw, ear, chin, cheek, eyes, nose

TIGER CLAW

Key: The tiger claw can be used for striking or scratching in a powerful whipping motion.

Targets: Frontal face, especially eyes and nose

Chapter 4
Elbow   Strikes

The elbow is an excellent weapon to use in close range combat because of its proximity to the upper body targets. It can move in many directions and still deliver a powerful strike because it is backed by the twisting force of the shoulder and hips. While commonly used for striking and thrusting, it also can be used for pushing in combination with a takedown.

The elbow moves on a horizontal or vertical plane. When traveling on a horizontal plane, force is created by twisting the body. The forearm or upper parts of the elbow are used for impact. When traveling on a vertical plane, force is maximized by using gravity and body weight. The strike is concentrated into the bony point of the elbow to create a precise and painful impact.

In both cases, the force of the elbow strike is originating from the large triangle created by the fist, elbow and shoulder at the start of the movement. As the elbow strike is executed, the triangle becomes smaller and smaller until it is tightly formed at the point of impact.

For example, when starting a horizontal hook, you open your shoulder and angle your elbow at about ninety degrees. As you progress to the target, your shoulder will begin to close and your fist and shoulder will come closer together. By the time you reach the target your fist and shoulder will be touching and your hips and shoulders will have rotated one hundred and eighty degrees.

This process uses many forces (elbow, shoulders, hip and fist) in conjunction with each other to make the elbow a devastating weapon.

ELBOW STRIKING

HORIZONTAL HOOK

Key: The horizontal hook makes maximum use of the torque of the hips and shoulders. It works best against a frontal attack by the opponent.

Targets: Jaw, rib cage, thigh

REVERSE HOOK

Key: The reverse hook travels in a circular path and creates impact with the back of the elbow. It works best against a lateral attack.

Targets: Neck, jaw, rib cage

SPINNING REVERSE HOOK

Key: The spinning reverse hook works on the same principle as the reverse hook but with a spin to the rear. It works best against rear attacks.

Targets: Jaw, rib cage

UPPERCUT

Key: The uppercut moves at an upward angle and works well against a lunging or ducking opponent.

Targets: Face, chin

VERTICAL STRIKE

Key: The vertical strike can be used to attack any horizontal plane on the opponent's body like the back of a bent over opponent or the thigh, when you trap an incoming kick.

Targets: Back, rear neck, collar bone, spine, thigh

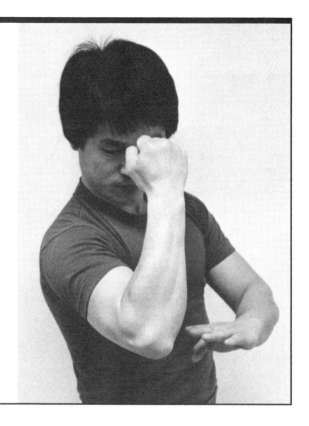

PUSH

Key: Elbow pushing is utilized in connection with a takedown technique, such as an outside takedown with an elbow push to the ribs. It can also be used to follow up after a grab or to push the opponent away to create distance for a medium or long range attack.

Targets: Face, neck, rib cage, thigh, back

ELBOW THRUST

SIDE THRUST

Key: The side thrust is used laterally against a flat, vertical plane on the opponent's body.

Targets: Rib cage, solar plexus, head, groin

REAR THRUST

Key: The rear thrust is used against an attack from behind.

Targets: Solar plexus, rib cage, groin

CHAPTER 5
KNEE STRIKES

The knee is used effectively in close combat against low section targets. A knee attack is helpful in freeing your upper body from the opponent's grip. If he is concentrating on a grappling strategy, a knee to the leg or groin will surprise him and distract him from his plan. A drop knee strike can also be used to finish an opponent. When the opponent is on the ground, concentrate your force into one knee and drop your body onto his body, creating a penetrating impact with your knee.

When striking, bend your knee tightly and use your hips to propel your knee to the target. Be cautious when striking hard objects with the knee because it is very vulnerable to joint and tissue damage. Use knee attacks against soft body areas like the groin, thigh muscle, and stomach.

STRAIGHT KNEE

Key: The straight knee moves forward on linear path to the target. It is good for ambush attacks or aggressive attackers.

Targets: Groin, stomach

VERTICAL KNEE

Key: The vertical knee strike moves in a forward and upward direction simultaneously. Use the vertical knee when you can pull the opponent's head or upper body downward into the range of your knee.

Targets: Face, stomach, groin

HORIZONTAL KNEE

Key: The horizontal knee moves on a horizontal plane with mechanics similar to the horizontal elbow hook.

Targets: Outer thigh, inner thigh, groin, ribs, stomach

DROP KNEE

Key: The drop knee uses gravity and your body weight to attack the fallen opponent.

Targets: Back, ribs, solar plexus, head

Chapter 6
Kicking Skills

Kicking requires special attention to balance and weight shifting, because you must balance your entire body weight on one leg during the execution of a kick. Standing on a single leg is very unnatural in terms of human body mechanics. Balancing on one leg is probably the most vulnerable position you will voluntarily assume in combat.

To minimize the risk of kicking emphasize posture, balance, body shifting, and a quick withdrawal of the leg in practice. Speed is also necessary to avoid having your leg grabbed or trapped or becoming the victim of a takedown.

Done properly, kicking is a relatively safe risk because you gain the added advantage of distance. The legs are the longest part of our anatomy and therefore perfect for long and medium range combat.

FRONT KICK

Key: The front kick is a simple linear kick that is best used against an opponent who is rushing in and presents a target on the front of his body.

Targets: Groin, shin, stomach, solar plexus, face (bending opponent)

SIDE KICK

Key: The side kick uses the knee joint to transfer the force created by the hip and the thrusting motion of the knee. It is primarily used to stop an invasion of your safety zone or to push away an attacker.

Targets: Knee, thigh, stomach, ribs, back, hip, shin

HOOK KICK

Key: The hook kick integrates the torque of the hips and the centripetal force of the foot. There are two types, the frontal circular hook kick and the reverse spin hook kick.

Targets: Knee, groin, thigh, stomach, rib cage, neck, head, calf, hip (rear), spine

BACK KICK

Key: The back kick uses mechanics similar to the side kick and is most effective against a rear attack.

Targets: Groin, stomach, thigh, knee, shin

CHAPTER 7
TAKEDOWNS AND THROWS

Takedowns and throws are a means of controlling your opponent and ending a confrontation cleanly. They also create space between you and your opponent so you can turn a close combat situation into a medium or long range fight.

Takedowns and especially throws, combine gravity and the impact of the ground to create a devastating blow. They work within the natural mechanics of the body to emphasize finesse over power. This is a big advantage if your opponent is bigger than you are. They are also designed to draw in the aggressor and use his momentum against him.

To execute throws and takedowns effectively, concentrate on developing timing, balance, weight shifting and gripping. These delicate skills require a great deal of practice with a partner because they depend on the interaction of two peoples' movements. Throws and takedowns are short range combat skills.

TAKEDOWNS

OUTSIDE TAKEDOWN

Key: For an outside takedown, step across your body and put your leg behind or next to the opponent's leg. Twist his upper body in the direction of your initial step and use your leg as leverage to topple him over.

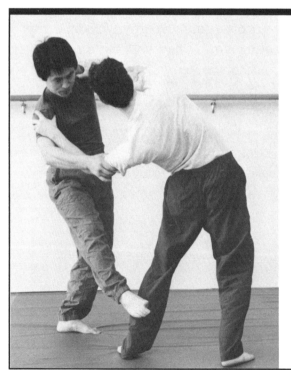

INSIDE SWEEP

Key: To execute an inside sweep, twist the opponent's upper body in one direction while sweeping his weight bearing leg in the opposite direction.

CROSS LEG TAKEDOWN

Key: A   cross   leg takedown uses your leg as an obstacle placed   in front of or behind the opponent's legs.   The obstacle stops his lower body   movement   but allows his upper body movement to continue with enough acceleration force to become top heavy and tip over. This is the same principle as tripping a person who is running.

SPIN TAKEDOWN

Key: A spin takedown requires a 180° turn to the rear, pivoting on the front foot, and executes the sweep with the rear foot. To   increase   the effectiveness, grab   the front of the opponent's upper body and push it in the opposite direction as your rear foot sweeps the front leg.   Spinning takedowns are used   in open stance.

REAR HOOK TAKEDOWN

Key: Position one hand behind the knee of the opponent and pull. Simultaneously, place the other hand on his chest and push. Create a circular coupling motion to take him down.

LATERAL HOOK TAKEDOWN

Key: Snap one hand on the lateral side of the opponent's knee and pull inward to the center of his body. Simultaneously snap the other hand on the opposite side of the chest and push.

THROWS

STATIC LEVERAGE

Key: In a static leverage throw, your leverage (center of gravity) does not move. Your leverage is momentarily fixed in one place for stability and you execute the throw by moving your arms and legs around the leverage. You become the center of the motion.

Examples: Hip throw, shoulder throw

DYNAMIC LEVERAGE

Key: In a dynamic leverage throw, your body moves with the throw. Create leading momentum by throwing your body in the direction of the throw and your opponent will follow the path of your movement. This throw makes full use of gravity and body weight.

Examples: Sacrifice throw, stomach throw

CHAPTER 8
JOINT IMMOBILIZATION

Joint immobilization techniques are those movements that cause hyperextension of one or more joints. Joint immobilization techniques tie up the opponents limbs and create such pain that he becomes unable to respond. Pain is created by pressing or twisting the joint in a direction in which it does not naturally move. For example, pressing the finger backward or twisting the elbow.

Joint immobilization is useful in short to medium range combat and ground combat for locking up or pinning an aggressor. The key to applying a joint locking technique successfully is to keep intensifying the pressure on the hyperextended joint and transforming the technique into a more effective one by moving continuously. This allows you to control the opponent's movements and avoid giving him an opening for an escape or reverse.

Joint immobilization is an excellent tool for controlling an assailant without inflicting the type of concussive damage caused by a strong strike or kick. Once the person is subdued, he can be released relatively unharmed. If, on the other hand, the assailant does not relent, the joint lock can be intensified to the point of dislocation.

Use caution in practicing joint locks. Everyone has a different ability to tolerate hyperextension of their joints. In some people, even slight pressure will result in an injury.

WRIST LOCK

Key: The wrist lock can be applied in five different ways: upward press, downward press, lateral press, outward twist and reverse twist. Each type puts pressure on the hand to manipulate the wrist.

ARM LOCK

Key: The arm lock can be applied in nine ways: upward elbow press, downward elbow press, side elbow press, inside arm lock, outside arm lock, straight in arm lock, V arm lock, spinning inward twist and spinning outward twist.

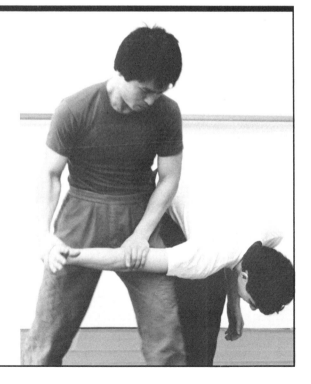

SHOULDER LOCK

Key: The shoulder lock has two variations: shoulder pin, and triangle arm press. Each type uses the arm to manipulate the shoulder joint into a hyperextended position

PINNING

Key: Pinning on the ground can be done by locking the arm, shoulder, head, or legs. A pin is any lock that immobilizes the entire body by applying pain to one or more joints.

BOOK THREE

STRATEGY and TACTICS

DEFENSIVE TACTICS

CHAPTER I
PRIMARY RESPONSE

Offense and Defense. Attack and Counterattack. These basic concepts of combat are familiar to even the most novice strategist. Perhaps too familiar. Have you ever taken the time to analyze the fundamental meaning of offense and defense? Offense is generally viewed as forward movement against the opponent. Defense as the retreat and regrouping. Attacking quantifies the actions taken during the forward moving offense and counterattacking encompasses the actions that fortify the retreat.

At the beginner and intermediate stages of fighting, these concepts are useful for their simplicity. They give the fighter a clear sequence of actions necessary to defeat the opponent.

As a fighter becomes more skilled, he begins to find offense that moves backward and forward, that side steps and even stands still. He finds defense that doesn't retreat.

To define the total concept of strategy, without the preconceived notions of offense and defense, think of it in terms of the primary response and the secondary response. The primary response is the segment of combat in which you neutralize your opponent. Neutralizing the opponent means destroying any advantage he has over you, establishing equal ground from which you can prevail. The primary response uses the conventional defensive tactic of stopping the advancing attack combined with the additional step of

selecting a skill that will create a weakness in the opponent's strategy for you to exploit.

When you have executed a successful primary response, the secondary response will follow naturally. It will take advantage of the neutralization and the vulnerability created by the primary response.

The primary response extinguishes the immediate threat posed by the opponent and the secondary response removes the potential threat.

THE PRIMARY RESPONSE

The primary response is rooted in the instinctive safety response with which all animals are born. Every animal has a distinct safety zone that should not be penetrated by perceived enemies. Consider a wild animal such as a deer or a rabbit. When approached by humans, the most common response is a hasty retreat. An unfamiliar person is seen as an intruder. Sensing he is no match for the intruder, the animal flees. Most animals will fight only as a last resort and then they will resolve to fight to the death.

As civilized humans, we have many more choices available to us than do rabbits and deer. Yet, our primary defense should still be the instinctive one: flight. We could not be the technological, industrialized world we are today if we still had to fight for every meal and defend our home from every passing stranger. Humans have implemented a very sophisticated system of criminal laws and moral rules to avoid conflict wherever possible. This is a complex extension of the individual safety response.

Unfortunately, our system is not fail-safe. Laws are broken with alarming regularity and moral codes differ from person to person, culture to culture. Therefore, it is often impossible to avoid conflict entirely.

When faced with an inevitable confrontation we have to respond in a way that will protect our bodies from harm and allow us to escape. When initial escape is impossible, direct physical action becomes necessary. Physical engagement can encompass anything from simply ducking a punch to controlling a knife wielding attacker. The initial actions used to avoid and remove an immediate threat are part of the primary response.

The main goal of the primary response is to neutralize the attack of the opponent and prepare to launch the secondary response. To do this effectively, you will need to establish four things in your favor in a split second:

1. Time

You can gain needed time by stunning your attacker into inaction or confusing his strategy. Use the time you gain to plan and execute your next movements. Every extra second is valuable time to prepare your secondary response.

2. Stability

When you are confronted, you are likely to lose your balance and composure at least momentarily. Psychological or physical instability creates additional openings for your opponent. By initiating a primary response, you will be able to regain a comfortable posture and prepare to attack. Now is the time to establish a strong but flexible position in preparation for your secondary response.

3. Superiority

Through an effective primary response, you can gain physical and mental superiority over your opponent. If you evade or block his attack, he will be momentarily unbalanced and discouraged. The mind controls the body and plays a large role in its ability to function at peak effectiveness. Defeating or discouraging your opponent psychologically will give you a significant advantage.

4. Opening

In addition to temporarily stopping the attacking opponent, an accurate primary response will create an opening for your secondary response. In this sense, the primary response and secondary response are not separate actions but complementary parts of the whole.

Let's look at an example of how these four qualities can be established. You are confronted by an opponent who is larger and stronger than you. He throws a wide right hook to your jaw. You duck, take one step inside his range and come up with a rear hook takedown. First by ducking, you create time to prepare your next move. Then by stepping forward into the range of his punch you cause him to miss while setting up your next attack. You are positioned low to the ground and have created a perfect opening for the takedown. Your attacker will be confused and distracted by your tactics and giving you an opportunity to follow up with your secondary response.

KEYS TO PRIMARY RESPONSE

1. Neutralize opponent's attack
2. Destroy opponent's force frame (line)

FOUR PRIMARY RESPONSES

All primary responses fit into one of four categories: evading, parrying, blocking, cutting-in.

EVADING: EMPTY THE SPACE

Evading can be thought of as ''emptying the space'' between you and your opponent. It is the surest way of maintaining your safety zone and it should always be your first choice. Evading is the most natural response to an unwanted intruder. You use it all the time, even in social situations. Imagine yourself having a conversation with a business acquaintance. The acquaintance leans too close to you and you instinctively step back. Though you do not perceive a physical threat, the invasion of your personal comfort zone puts your subconscious on alert.

Your comfort zone differs from one situation to another. In your home or among friends, your comfort zone is relaxed or nonexistent. In familiar but high pressure environments like school or work, it is an active barometer of whom to trust and how much trust to place in them. In unfamiliar or threatening surroundings, the comfort zone is buffered by a larger safety zone. Anyone crossing into your perceived safety zone is seen as a potential threat, therefore you unconsciously move to put them back outside your safety zone.

Evasion occurs every day on many levels. Evading is based on instinct and judgment. In combat, your initial reaction should be to evade the confrontation entirely. When this fails, try to evade the

Evasion

Forms of Evasion: ducking, jumping, weaving, withdrawing, back step, avoiding, forward step, rolling, angular step, dropping, shifting

physical blows of the aggressor. Evasion must be total to be successful. Partial evasion will result in some damage to you and superiority for your attacker.

The choice to use evasion is based primarily on the amount of force your opponent has relative to your strength. If your opponent has a high force advantage, evasion may be your only choice. Imagine a car coming at you at fifty miles per hour. Would you even consider blocking it?

Because of its variable nature, evasion is advantageous for the person who is small, quick, instinctive and has good body movement and footwork. It requires a minimum of effort to get maximum results.

PARRYING: REDIRECT THE FORCE

Parrying is done by redirecting the force of an approaching attack. For any given attack there is a single point in time and space at which the parry can work. This point is determined by the type of attack and the type of parry used. If your opponent throws a right straight punch to your face, parry with your left hand moving from right to left.

As the attacker begins his punch, anticipate the speed and direction of the strike. Time your parry to strike his forearm before his fist reaches its target. By slightly pushing his forearm, you redirect the path of the strike away from your body. The amount of force required for parrying is less than that of blocking because you allow the power of the strike to dissipate in the air rather than impact your body. The key to parrying is to allow the technique to follow its natural course with only minor alteration. The more you try to change the path of the strike, the more energy you will expend which can cause your body to become overextended.

Parrying requires practice to develop the required anticipation and timing. Practice recognizing the initial movements of common attacks. By sensing the type of strike your opponent will use, you can gain added time to prepare your response. When you identify an impending attack, time your parry so it meets the attack just before it hits your body. The point of contact should be inside the terminal of the striking weapon. If the attack is a punch, parry the forearm. If it is a kick, parry the shin. If it is an elbow strike, parry the bicep and so forth.

Types of parries

Upward	linear
	angular - inward and outward
	circular - inward and outward
Downward	linear
	angular - inward and outward
	circular - inward and outward
Lateral	linear - right and left
	circular - right and left

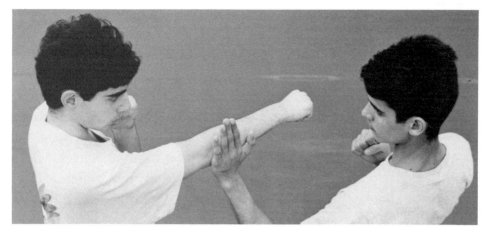

Parrying

The amount of contact required for parrying varies with the type of attack. Generally a smooth guiding, slipping or pushing motion is used. Most parries are done with the hand, but the arm, shin and foot also can be used. Hand and arm parries are safest because the upper body can be shifted out of the line of attack while the hand or arm executes the parry. Leg and foot parries requires you to maintain a fixed position on one leg while the other leg goes to work. Balancing on one leg puts you at considerable risk for a damaging counterattack.

Parrying can take the form of upward, downward or lateral movements to complement the direction of the attack. Each type of parry can be varied as linear, angular or circular.

Parrying is most effective against linear attacks because the path of a straight attack is easy to anticipate and disrupt. Against circular attacks, parrying becomes more difficult.

Principally, parrying is best suited to people with quick reflexes and a good sense of timing. Use parrying to defeat powerful attacks whose blows are too damaging to stop head on.

Keys to Parrying

1. Anticipate the attack
2. Select the parry that requires the least change of direction of the attack
3. Parry inside the terminal of the striking weapon
4. Time your parry to minimize the amount of force needed

BLOCKING: EXTINGUISHING THE FORCE

A block is a movement that forcefully interrupts the opponent's attack, thereby extinguishing it. Blocking is an aggressive, initiative action that requires commitment. It is most useful against evenly matched or smaller opponents because in blocking, force is met with force and the stronger person will likely win.

Because blocking naturally creates opposition by the opponent, immediately follow a block with a series of finishing blows. If you fail in initiating a quick secondary response, you risk an aggressive counter attack by your opponent.

Blocking, like parrying, is often done with the hands and forearms. Blocks are described by the section of the body to which they are applied (high section, low section, and middle section) or by the direction of the application of force (inward, outward, upward, or downward). They also can be classified as straight or circular.

Types of blocks

High section	inward - straight and circular
	outward - straight and circular
	upward - straight and circular
Middle section	inward - straight and circular
	outward - straight and circular
	upward - straight and circular
	downward - straight and circular
Low section	inward - straight and circular
	outward - straight and circular
	upward - straight and circular
	downward - straight and circular

Leg blocks are useful for stopping attacks to the legs and lower trunk, however they require speed and anticipation. Beyond the commonly practiced arm and leg blocks, there are several uncommon but highly effective blocks such as the V block.

BLOCKING VS. PARRYING

In combat, correctly choosing between blocking and parrying can significantly enhance the effectiveness of your defense. Here are some guidelines for selecting the correct tactic.

Blocking and parrying versus linear attacks

Parrying is used to defend against linear attacks (any attack moving toward the body on a single plane). Some examples of linear attacks are side kick, straight punch, finger jab, and other stabbing and thrusting attacks. Linear attacks are aimed at the center line of the body and designed to penetrate vital areas to cause maximum damage.

Because penetrating strikes are the most dangerous types of attacks, they require careful consideration. Parrying, combined with evading, is the safest combination for diffusing linear attacks. First by evading, you move your center line out of range of the attack. Second, by parrying, you avoid meeting the penetrating force head on. Instead you can sweep it aside and allow its energy to dissipate in the air. Even if your evasion or parry is not fully successful, you are more likely to be damaged on your less vulnerable extremities, than the intended center line targets.

Blocking a linear attack is dangerous because you must create a strong foundational stance to meet force with force. If you are unsuccessful, your center line is vulnerable and your stance is inflexible. Once your opponent breaks through your blocking defense, he will continue to deliver his blows until he reaches his intended target. As you can see in Fig 3.1 the linear blow is more likely to break the plane of defense in blocking than in parrying. Parrying creates a ricochet effect, deflecting the force with less effort and damage.

Fig 3.1

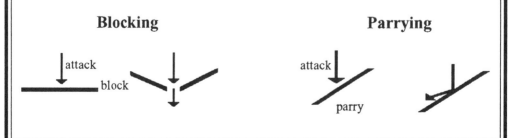

Parrying and blocking versus a circular attack

Parrying depends on estimating the line of attack and redirecting it with little effort. This is relatively simple to do with linear attacks because they travel in a single direction from start to finish. The defender needs only to position himself on one side of the path of the strike and redirect it to the opposing direction.

However, circular attacks travel in an arc toward their target. Because of the centripetal force and speed created by circular attacks it is difficult to redirect their line of motion. The main reason being that the perfect point of contact between a parry and a circular attack lies at only one point in time and space. If you miss parrying the attack at the exact point of contact or at the correct time, you are sure to be hit.

Fig 3.2

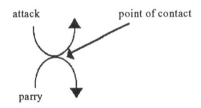

Parry of circular attack

The exacting nature of parrying a circular attack is risky and requires a disproportionate amount of effort for actual combat.

In   defending against a circular attack,   evading is preferred. However, evading is not always possible. When contact is inevitable, blocking is most useful. Circular attacks are primarily directed at the outside circumference of the body. Circular attacks include the hook kick and punch, the backfist, the whipping tiger claw, and other slashing and whipping movements.

The natural course of circular attacks makes them better suited for blocking because blocking creates a barricade between the attack and the target. However, this barricade is not intended to meet the full force of the attack, which is carried by the terminal point of the attacking weapon, but to interrupt the center of the attacking arc as illustrated in Fig. 3.3.

This idea is tantamount to entering the eye of the hurricane. The hurricane spins violently on its central axis, but the axis itself is calm and can be entered without damage. To experiment with this concept, imagine a small steel ball attached to the end of a rope. If another person acts as the axis and spins the string in a circle, the ball will gather greater speed and force with each rotation. If you attempt to block the ball, you will sustain at least some damage to your arm. However, if you step inside the orbit of the ball and grab the string to which it is fastened, you will safely stop the ball from spinning.

Fig 3.3

attack

block

Block of circular attack

This is the principle of blocking a circular attack. Enter the orbit of the terminal (the foot, hand, weapon) and contact the arcing body midway between the terminal and the axis on which it is rotating. The possible contact points are anywhere between the terminus and axis, however, the midpoint is safest. To master blocking, practice stepping-in or sliding-in footwork perfect timing.

Once you understand and implement the proper function of blocking and parrying, your defense will become impenetrable.

CUT-IN: FILL THE SPACE

The final tactic available for the primary response is the cut-in defense. Cutting an attack can be thought of as filling the space intended for the path of the attack. For example, if your opponent launches a hook kick and you lunge toward him, into the arc of the kick, you have filled the space he intended to use for his kick. Now he can no longer finish his attack.

There are five classes of cut-in defenses:

1. Circular cut-in vs. circular attack

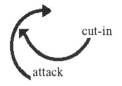

2. Circular cut-in vs. linear attack

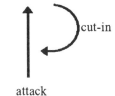

3. Straight cut-in vs. two pronged attack

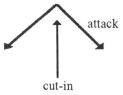

4. Low cut-in vs. high attack

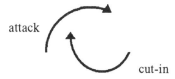

5. High cut-in vs. low attack

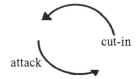

Cut-in Defense

Cutting an attack is most useful when you can read the opponent's action beforehand or when it is too late to employ any of the previous responses. It also requires the opportunity to move into the arc of the attack (the eye of the hurricane) and cut the attack at the trunk or root. This is easier if the opponent is bigger and has a longer range than you.

Cutting an attack is part of the classic guerrilla strategy of sending a few elite commandos to attack the headquarters of the enemy. This causes the nerve center of the force to become unbalanced and sends the extremities into disarray.

You can apply this to one-on-one combat by cutting the attack, penetrating the opponent's defense and striking his vital targets. Then immediately retreat to your safety zone and await another chance. Never stay within the opponent's reach for more time than it takes for him to recover his composure.

Cut-in responses include jamming, cut-in blocks, circular cutting, straight cutting, ducking in, and kicking cuts. Cutting also can take the form of an initiative attack. Any movement that fills the space between you and your opponent and hinders his ability to attack can be defined as a cut-in.

Cutting the opponent's attack requires good footwork, body shifting, timing and guts.

CHAPTER 2
SECONDARY RESPONSE

The secondary response is defined as all the actions necessary to end a confrontation. This encompasses all means of escape, from fighting back to running away. Most confrontations will involve some combination of the two since not all fights end like in the movies, with the bad guy lying on the ground and the good guy riding into the sunset.

Real life is much more complex and often more messy. You will rarely escape a physical confrontation unharmed. The key is to do more damage to your opponent than he does to you.

Damage control is established by the primary response and maintained throughout the secondary response. Once you have neutralized your opponent's initial attack, move immediately to your secondary response. Time is a critical ally at this stage. The duration of neutrality may last less than a second and whoever claims superiority during this time is likely to be the victor.

What you choose for your secondary response depends on the situation. It may be something you have practiced or it may be something you never thought of before. Be flexible. Flexibility wins where rigidity fails.

In choosing your secondary response, consider your power, accuracy and timing in addition to individual skills. Power is a delicate subject in combat arts. Too much or too little power can upset the timing and accuracy of your attack. Gauge the amount of force necessary to finish an assailant and apply exactly that much. Using the necessary amount of power allows you to maximize your speed, agility and timing. Without these qualities, you will be exerting your incredibly powerful blows in the air.

For your power to be effective, it must contact the chosen target at the correct time. This is where accuracy and timing become important. Accuracy is essential in the secondary response. If you select your targets with care and strike them correctly, the effectiveness of your blows will increase. Accuracy is especially important when attacking vital points like the throat, jaw and back of the knee. An off-target strike will still cause damage, but not nearly the amount you intended. A slight miscalculation will force you to continue to attack until you strike a more precise blow.

Besides good accuracy and power, timing is required. Timing is the ability to cause two moving bodies to collide at the correct point in space and time relative to each other. The odds of this happening by accident are clearly not in your favor. However, you can increase your odds through practice. Timing is dependent on reflexes, speed, and mental quickness. Each of these contributes to your ability to react quickly and accurately.

SELECTING A SECONDARY RESPONSE

Timing, accuracy, power and a correct primary response are all prerequisites to the secondary response, but they alone will not insure your success. The secondary response is based on your ability to respond to the current situation as it presents itself and to make split second decisions based on ever changing data.

There are several important principles governing the secondary response. Understanding them will help you make strategic decisions with a minimum of conscious thought. The first principle is to understand the mechanics of the human body and its interaction with its surroundings. There are scientific and natural laws that dictate much of what we are able to accomplish with our bodies and how our bodily parts interact within each movement.

Understanding these laws will help you to choose techniques and tactics wisely. For example, you have a good idea how much strength, speed, flexibility, and power you can produce. Adrenaline may allow you to increase your output somewhat during combat, but these attributes will remain relatively constant. By knowing your limitations, you can eliminate certain skills that are not possible for you to use effectively. While you may still practice them to improve personally, avoid them in actual combat.

In addition to physical mechanics, there are combat mechanics. Combat mechanics encompass the laws that govern physical confrontations. Throughout human history many lifetimes have been devoted to studying military and combat strategy. There is much to be learned from what others have proven to be both true and untrue.

Throughout this book are strategies and tactics that are universally true. Apply these to your own training to simplify the amount of conscious thought and trial-and-error experimentation required in your free combat practice.

Exceptions, however, are bound to occur. If you use a technique a hundred times, you may get the same response ninety-eight times and be totally surprised by the other two. How you handle the exceptions will determine your ultimate success or failure. Never assume your opponent will respond as planned.

Foe example, you throw a straight punch expecting your opponent to block or parry it. You then plan to follow with a low section kick and take down. Imagine your surprise when your opponent, instead of reacting as expected, rushes right by your punch and applies a choke hold. Your brain is already confined by its plan to go forward with the low kick and you find yourself confused and frustrated. Sensing your mental lapse, your opponent easily pins you and you are left defenseless.

This mistake is made by even the most skilled combatants. Having a plan is good, but being confined by the plan is not. Always be prepared to change on a moment's notice. If you are a novice strategist, develop a basic format and learn how to be a free thinker as you progress. Selecting the right tool for the job and remaining flexible are your best weapons.

SECONDARY COMBINATIONS

So far, the emphasis of the secondary response has been on the ability to follow up the primary response with a correct and well executed technique. Occasionally, one perfect skill may be enough to end a conflict, but this is unusual. A single technique will only be effective if it is perfect in all attributes and if your opponent is similar in size, skill and strength.

In most cases, you need a combination of well placed strikes, throws, locks, etc. to win. Combining techniques is the next step in building an arsenal of combat skills.

I. QUANTITATIVE PRINCIPLES OF COMBINATIONS

Single Techniques

To work, single techniques require perfection in all attributes . The perfect attributes for each single skill are covered in the fundamentals section. In addition to the basic characteristics of each technique, you will find many of your own ways to improve them according to your style and skill level. Your adaptation is just as important to your development as the learned aspects of each   movement. Before you attempt adaptation, consider the purpose of the movement and understand its usage and character. Adaptation should truly improve on the skill, not just change it for the sake of change.

Multiple Techniques

Multiple techniques are often necessary to end a conflict success- fully. A follow-up technique may be needed to strengthen an initial attack or a second blow can intensify the effect of the first. Whatever the case, there are two principal ways of combining skills in multiple attacks, by force and by direction.

2. DIRECTIONAL PRINCIPLES OF COMBINATIONS

A directional classification defines your movement in relation to the position of your opponent. Direction is an obvious and external quality of a combination. We can easily see it and it is rarely deceptive. There are two types of directional classifications: lateral and planar.

Lateral Combination

Lateral combinations are those that attack the sides of the opponent alternately or randomly. They are primarily combinations of circular movements including striking, kicking, throwing, locking and takedowns. They can consist of any combination of high-low, foot-foot, hand-foot or hand-hand attacks.

Lateral combinations work well for fighters with good mobility and speed. Their randomness confuses and frustrates opponents, especially those who are big or slow. When forming lateral combinations, include variety in the type of skills, and the height and direction of approach.

Planar Combination

Planar combinations are combinations that attack the opponent on a single plane running through his body from front to back. A plane can run directly through the center line or at a slight angle to the right or left. The only requirement is that all movements are consistent in their line of approach.

Planar combinations consist of penetrating and thrusting linear attacks to the center line of the body including punching, jabbing, linear kicks, knee thrusts, back fists, and tackling. Planar attacks are meant to do serious damage by aiming for vital targets such as the face, spine, groin and internal organs. Create quick techniques and develop total body shifting to take advantage of and penetrate openings on the center line.

Planar attacks also can be combined in groups of high-low approaches with foot-foot, hand-foot or hand-hand skills.

LATERAL COMBINATION

Right hook punch   **Left hook kick**   **Right tiger claw**

PLANAR COMBINATION

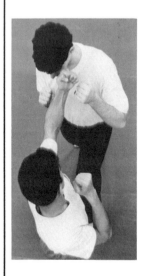

Left backfist   **Head Butt**   **Right vertical knee**

3. FORCE PRINCIPLE OF COMBINATIONS

Force classifications are defined by the path or paths over which they apply force to the opponent. Consequently, they are often more difficult to identify than directional classifications. Force is an internal characteristic that is not readily evident to an observer. It can be obvious, as in unified force or deceptive as in opposing force.

Unified Force Combinations

Unified force combinations are groups of skills that apply continuous force in a single direction. Every strike serves to magnify the effect of the previous one. Strikes can be the same such as a flurry of punches to the body or they can be diverse like a variety of linear and circular kicks aimed at the legs of the opponent.

Unified force combines high-low-middle approaches to linear and circular attacks with all parts of the body. The only qualifying factor is that every blow will deliver its force in the same direction as the previous one. This punishes the opponent in one area and wears him down faster. Unified force combinations are effective in prolonged combat because they have a greater effect over time.

Circular Force Combinations

Circular force combinations are combinations that apply force that rotates around an axis. The axis is located at a point on your body, that is close to your center of gravity. The force is then directed to the target by two terminal points on your body, usually your hands or feet. The resulting effect is the magnification of both applications of force.

The first application of force, whether by striking or grappling, will always intensify the second. In striking, the second strike is intensified by the centripetal force generated by the first. For example, a backfist to the face, followed by a hook kick to the leg and a back kick to the groin will create a continuous 360 degree circle with one technique leading directly into and intensifying the next.

So, in striking, one movement follows the other in smooth and complementary progression. In grappling, however, the movement pattern is different. When applying a throwing or locking skill, the circular force will occur concurrently, with each force simultaneously intensifying the other. An example is a rear hook takedown where one hand pushes the upper body of the opponent backward and the other pulls the knee forward.   For maximum results, the pulling and pushing movements must be done simultaneously with a sensitivity to the circular force being created.

Opposing Force Combinations

Opposing force combinations are pairs of skills that apply force in antagonistic directions.   They consist of at least two distinct movements that work in opposition to each other, yet are complementary. They often look similar to circular force combinations but there is a conspicuous distinction. Circular force skills can be traced to a single line of movement around one axis. Opposing force skills move in intersecting lines or arcs.

Like circular combinations, opposing force combinations can be studied in terms of striking skills and grappling skills. Opposing force strikes are often used to set each other up. An example is a left hook punch to the head followed by a right hook punch to the head. The left hook will start the opponent's head moving to the right. When you follow with the right hook, the force created by the left hook, combined with the weight of your opponent, will crash into the force of your right hook, to increase the damage done. By using the left hook as a set-up, you intensify the effect of the main technique, the right hook.

In grappling, you also can use an antecedent technique to set up the main technique. For example, by pulling your opponent to the left you cause him to resist in the opposite direction, to the right. When he has firmly set his center of gravity to the right, change your tactic and take him down to the right. Use his resistance against him and reduce the amount of effort necessary to defeat him.

To summarize, in striking, increase the force of the second technique by preceding it with an opposing force strike. In grappling, apply force in one direction, then reverse the direction of the force and use your opponent's resistance against him.

UNIFIED FORCE COMBINATION

Throw by gripping the shoulders and pulling to the right with your right hand and pushing to the right with your left hand

CIRCULAR FORCE COMBINATION

Right palm push and left hand hook for a takedown

OPPOSING FORCE COMBINATION

**Twisting wrist lock to the right followed by reverse
twisting wrist lock to the left**

COMBINING FORCE AND DIRECTIONAL PRINCIPLES

Every combination can be defined by both force and direction. It may not always be obvious at first, but careful study will reveal which category the skills fit into.   Here are some examples of combinations from each force/direction category:

Lateral unified: Right hook kick to the thigh and right elbow hook to the face

Lateral circular: Left whipping tiger claw to the face and left outside takedown

Lateral opposing: Right hook to the head and left hook to the head

Planar unified: Right side pushing kick to the thigh, left front kick to the body and right straight punch to the face

Planar circular: Right chin push and left hand hook the knee for a takedown

Planar opposing: Left hand grab behind the neck and right palm push/strike to the face and pull the head down into right vertical knee strike

These are the basic theories behind the secondary response. In upcoming sections of Book 3 and Book 4, you will learn about the strategic nuances of the secondary response in more depth.

CHAPTER 3
COMBINED RESPONSE

Now that you understand the function of the primary and secondary responses, let's look at how to combine them correctly. In theory, any primary response can be combined with any secondary response. (Fig 3.4) In reality, though, every combination will not work for every situation or every person. Choose your combined responses according to your skills, surroundings, opponent, the anticipated attack, and the flux of the confrontation.

Besides using your instinct and judgment there are two rules to consider:

1) Does the combination follow your natural body mechanics?

2) Does the combination protect your vital points satisfactorily?

Follow your natural body mechanics to ease the work load on your body during execution. Take full advantage of the laws of nature in combat. If you are large, capitalize on the size and power of your body. If you are small, emphasize quickness and deceptiveness. If you are flexible, use your wide range of motion to your advantage. Conversely, if you are not very flexible, don't make your body work extra hard by attempting high kicks. Work within your means and economize.

Fig 3.9

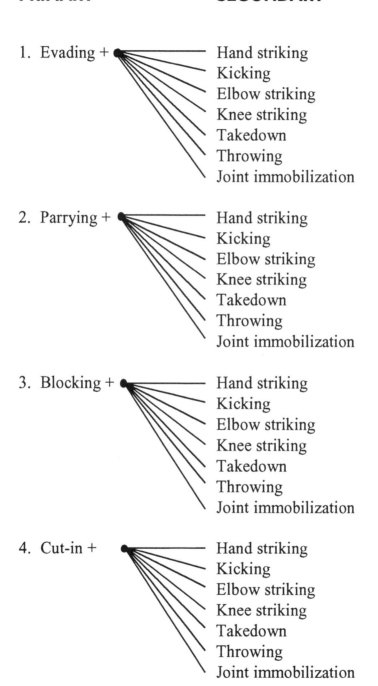

PRIMARY	SECONDARY

1. Evading +
- Hand striking
- Kicking
- Elbow striking
- Knee striking
- Takedown
- Throwing
- Joint immobilization

2. Parrying +
- Hand striking
- Kicking
- Elbow striking
- Knee striking
- Takedown
- Throwing
- Joint immobilization

3. Blocking +
- Hand striking
- Kicking
- Elbow striking
- Knee striking
- Takedown
- Throwing
- Joint immobilization

4. Cut-in +
- Hand striking
- Kicking
- Elbow striking
- Knee striking
- Takedown
- Throwing
- Joint immobilization

Protect your vital points at all times. Except for tactical reasons, avoid exposing potential targets to your opponent. If you must expose a vital target, move quickly and be prepared to counter attack before your opponent takes advantage of the opening.

> ### Keys in Primary-Secondary Combinations
>
> 1. Natural body mechanics
> 2. Natural laws of combat
> 3. Take advantage of physical strengths
> 4. Works within your limits
> 5. Economize

THE COMBINED RESPONSE

The combination of primary and secondary response is called the combined response. In the combined response there are four segments. Each segment has a specific goal and function in ending the confrontation. Sometimes the segments overlap and sometimes they may be repeated.

The ultimate combined response includes all of the four segments in a single movement. Here, secondary and primary response become one. This is rare but always possible, especially as you progress in skill level.

The first segment is the **initiation technique**. This is usually the primary response. The initiation technique uses the minimum force necessary to protect the body and engage the opponent. If your opponent attacks first, your initiating technique can be any one of the four primary responses. If you attack first, your initiating technique is a cut-in. Remember, a cut-in is any movement that fills the space between you and your opponent and interrupts your opponent's attack. It can be offensive or defensive.

The second segment of the combined response is a **transitional movement** that connects the primary response to the main technique of the secondary response. The transitional movement capitalizes on the neutral balance of power created by the primary response.

There are several ways of using the transitional movement:

1. To unbalance the opponent
   ex.: pull, push, grab or strike the opponent to make his stance unstable
2. To confuse the opponent
   ex.: feint an attack to cause your opponent to commit to a futile defense
3. To intensify your next technique
   ex.: initiate a line of force (circular, opposing, unified) to set up your main attack

The goal of the transitional movement is to create a bridge between establishing neutrality and establishing control of the fight. Use it to soften up or weaken the opponent for the main attack.

Once you have bridged the gap and created an opening, move to your main technique. The **main technique** is the one that all of the others exist for. It is the most damaging and effective weapon in your arsenal. The transitional and initiation segments will provide the opportunity for you to execute your plan of attack perfectly. Select a main technique that is powerful and fail-safe. Stick to your strongest skills, the ones you can rely on to get the job done.

When your main technique is completed, move quickly to the **finishing application**. By applying a finishing blow or hold, you ensure that the confrontation ends in your favor and the opponent is truly no longer a threat. The finishing technique can be defined in three ways:

1. Allows you to escape
2. Damages the opponent so he is unable to respond
3. Pins or immobilizes the opponent

A finishing application will decisively end the confrontation and allow you to escape if necessary.

COMBINED RESPONSE

Segment	Goal	Types	Examples
1. Initiation	1. Protect the body 2. Engage the opponent 3. Neutralize the opponent's force	Block Evade Cut-in Parry	V-Block duck punch jam kick redirect grab
2. Transition	1. Smooth flow between initiation and main 2. Turn the balance of power in your favor	unbalance confuse intensify	push finger jab to eyes grab the arm
3. Main	1. Damage the opponent so he cannot respond 2. End opponent's attack	Strike Kick Throw Takedown Lock Guerilla	elbow to jaw knee to groin side kick to knee sacrifice throw circular takedown lock & break arm Strike to eyes
4. Finishing	1. Decisively end the confrontation in your favor 2. Ensure your complete safety	Escape Pin Strike	run away to safety pin on ground strike to head

The initiation, transitional, main and finishing techniques can be separate movements or several of them may be found in a single move. Each segment may require more than one or two actions to complete. The initiating and transitional skills can be a series of four or five or more actions that set up the main attack. With your opponent actively working against you to prevent your main attack, you have to outsmart him as well as overpower him.

Here are some examples of how the four segments of a confrontation can be combined against similar attacks.

1. Opponent: Punching attack
   Defender: Evade + Parry + Grab + Throw + Escape
          (I)   (T)   (T)   (M)   (F)
   This sequence requires two transitional techniques because you cannot throw the opponent without first getting a firm grip on him. You also cannot grab him without first making contact in some way. By parrying his punch, you avoid his attack and set up your grab and throw. A hard throw onto a solid surface will provide you with time to continue attacking or escape.

2. Opponent: Punching attack
   Defender: Block + Backfist to face + Takedown + Pin
                  (I)   (T)   (M)   (F)
   Here is different response to a similar attack. If the
   opponent is comparable in skill to you, block his attack
   and launch a backfist to the face to stun him and close
   the distance. This will distract him, allowing you to
   move in for a takedown and pin.

3. Opponent: Pushing attack
   Defender: Cut-in + Knee to groin + Escape
            (I & T)   (M)   (F)
   When your opponent rushes at you, meet him half way
   to stifle his attack. This cutting technique is an initiating
   movement that obstructs the attack of your opponent, as
   well as a transitional skill that allows you to take the
   balance of your opponent and come into range for your
   main attack, a knee strike.

4. Opponent: Thrusting attack
   Defender: Block + Grab + Arm lock
              (I)   (T)   (M & F)

Against a thrusting attack, you block the thrust and grab the opponent. This time, you are able to execute your main and finishing techniques in one movement by applying an arm lock that leaves you opponent unable to respond.

5. Opponent: Kicking attack
   Defender: Hook kick to groin
              (I & T & M & F)

This defense, if delivered with power and accuracy, combines all four segments in one. Your opponent attacks with a kick, leaving his groin exposed and his balance vulnerable. You immediately deliver a full power kick to the groin intending to incapacitate him. This defense must be perfectly timed to avoid getting kicked, because you are not using any evasion or blocking movements. This is a cut-in primary response and a kicking secondary response consolidated.

Based on what you have learned in this section, consider the function of the primary and secondary response as it applies to your personal style of combat. Define what types of movements will work best for you and when you can use them most effectively.

Next look at the possible combinations of your top choices. Select a few that seem most effective and practice them intensively. These will be your core responses. Having a group of standard reactions will help you to be more spontaneous. Don't depend on them, just use them as a springboard from which you can adapt naturally if the chance arises. As you become more experienced, you will depend on your core techniques less and less. Until then, have something to rely on in an emergency.

PRIMARY/SECONDARY RESPONSE NOTES

1. My top 5 primary response skills:
   1. _____
   2. _____
   3. _____
   4. _____
   5. _____

2. My top 5 secondary response skills:

   Transition
   1. _____
   2. _____
   3. _____
   4. _____
   5. _____

   Main
   1. _____
   2. _____
   3. _____
   4. _____
   5. _____

   Finish
   1. _____
   2. _____
   3. _____
   4. _____
   5. _____

3. My top 5 combined responses:
   1. _____
   2. _____
   3. _____
   4. _____
   5. _____

OFFENSIVE
TACTICS

CHAPTER 4
DIRECT ATTACK

The best method of attacking is to use a direct attack from the beginning of the confrontation. When you see an opening, attack. This is the most basic principle of combat. It is also the most bold and risky type of offense.

A direct attack prevents your opponent from studying you and preparing an attack. Once you initiate a direct attack, do not allow any chance for recovery. Continue attacking until you finish the fight. The direct attack is used to stun the opponent into inaction and create openings to finish him.

The best time for a direct attack is before the opponent has a chance to launch his preferred offense. When he is planning to attack, hesitating, or trying to figure out your style, take action immediately to prevent him from getting the initiative.

Best time for a direct attack

When the opponent is:
1. Hesitating
2. Planning his attack
3. Studying your style

SINGLE DIRECT ATTACK

The direct attack is executed swiftly and economically. It takes the shortest, most direct path to the target without extraneous movements. Successful execution requires superior speed, agility and focus to penetrate the opponent's defense without being blocked. There are seven stages in the advancing action of a direct attack.

7 stages of direct attack

1. **Preparation**: relaxed but poised
2. **Initiation**: explosive speed
3. **Acceleration**: speed up smoothly
4. **Impact**: total concentration of power
5. **Follow-through**: release the force
6. **Withdrawal**: natural mechanics return the weapon to its original place
7. **Recovery**: return to strong stance with good defense

Each of these steps takes place in a split second or less. When you practice any attacking movement, be conscious of each step as it applies to the technique. Be totally involved in each phase of the action as it occurs without hurrying or skipping ahead.

To practice a right leg hook kick for a direct attack, first relax the muscles of your leg and torso. Then focus on your hips to create the initiation speed necessary. Accelerate by throwing your knee, followed by your foot, to the target. Upon impact, focus all of your power into your foot for maximum effect. Follow through with your knee and hip to release the power generated by your turning movement. When the force has been transferred to the target, allow your knee to snap your foot back to the chamber position and then return to a strong stance with your guard up and ready for the next attack.

This is the sequence of a perfect hook kick. As you can see, there are many factors involved in the hook kick besides the obvious action of the leg. To achieve optimum force and speed, the hips, knee and foot are the focus of the kick at different stages in the action. As you practice attacking, determine the specific part of the body that is the focus of each stage of the action. Work slowly through the movement until you execute each segment automatically.

Keys to single direct attack
1. Speed
2. Agility
3. Focus

Before initiating a direct attack in combat, there are three factors to check. First, measure the distance you must cover to attack effectively. Second, judge the type of opening presented and select the attack that best fits the opening. Third, estimate the possible responses of the opponent based on the actions he has used thus far. Is he a counter attacker or a retreater? Prepare accordingly.

Prepare for a direct attack by:

1. Checking the distance
2. Matching the opening with the correct attack
3. Estimating the opponent's response

Finally, when you have gathered the necessary data, attack according to your instinct and without hesitation. Instinct is not as vague as you might think. It is actually a summary of the intangible observations your subconscious is making about your surroundings. The actions of your opponent send many signals that you are not consciously aware of, but which affect your feeling about the opponent. If you feel confident in attacking, you are picking up signals that your opponent is vulnerable. If you feel hesitant, perhaps it is better to look more closely at what your opponent's actions are telling you.

Rely on instinct when you have difficulty deciding what course of action to take.

SIMULTANEOUS DIRECT ATTACK

If you miss the chance to attack first, and your reflexes are quick, you can still use a direct attack . As soon as the opponent begins his attack, attack to any available opening. The attack must be simultaneous with your opponent's or even a split second before. This is called a simultaneous direct attack.

Simultaneous attacking requires a good sense of combat, being able to spot the opponent's first signal of an upcoming attack. It also requires excellent reflexes and confidence in your ability. To attack an advancing opponent takes guts and skill. Practice for simultaneous and direct attacks with the determination of a hungry animal chasing its prey. When an animal senses a kill for food, it has no fear, only a single goal of getting the food.

Prerequisites for a simultaneous direct attack

1. Sense of combat
2. Reflexes
3. Confidence
4. Fortitude

First, practice simultaneous attacking with only the goal of contacting the opponent in mind. Once you are able to make contact with an attacking partner, practice refining each technique. Learn how to spot the start of an attack and how to find openings quickly according to the type of attack. Constantly work to overcome the natural apprehensive reaction to a physical threat.

When an opponent becomes the victim of your direct or simultaneous attack, he will be hesitant to attack again. Use direct attacks to psychologically, as well as, physically defeat your opponent.

CHAPTER 5
INDIRECT   ATTACK

An indirect attack is safer and more intricate than a direct or simultaneous attack. If a direct attack is the first dimension of combat, an indirect attack is the second . In a direct attack, you are the obvious initiator. In an indirect attack, you are the covert initiator. Indirect attacking is not reacting to the opponent as in counterattacking; it is making the opponent react to you and then taking advantage of his predictable response.

You create an opening and then attack it. There are three common types of indirect attacks: the feint, the draw and the set-up.

FEINTING

Feinting is widely used, not only in personal combat, but also in large scale war. The main idea of feinting is to give an empty or false movement, make the opponent respond and take advantage of the opening that his reaction creates. This opening can be anywhere including the front, side, back of the trunk, legs, arms, head, etc. Be prepared to respond to any opportunity, not just the one you logically expect to appear.

The most common way to create a feinting motion is to make a quick jerky motion with the hands or feet as you attack. The opponent will be distracted by the motion, assuming it is the point of initiation. While he focuses on your feint, launch your real attack.

A similar method is to use your eyes to feint. Look high and attack low or look low and attack high. This works only if the opponent is watching you intently and is therefore deceived by your eye movement. Don't depend on this tactic too heavily, use it sparingly.

A lesser known feint is to move unusually slowly and then speed up when your opponent tries to adjust. Create an atmosphere of slowness through your movements. The opponent will assume you are checking his response and will respond in kind. When you see he has psychologically adjusted to the slow movement, attack quickly and without hesitation. Another slow feint is to start a technique slower than normal and then accelerate as you near the target. Experiment with different combinations of speed and distance.

Finally, there is the psychological feint. Trap your opponent into making an incorrect assumption about your condition. If you appear to be tired or injured, he will assume you are defeated and will attack with less than full speed or power. If you look distracted there will be one of two possible responses by your opponent. Either he will take your distraction as a chance to have a momentary break or he will attack. If the former occurs, attack immediately. If his response is the latter, move and counter.

Sequence of Feinting

1. Give a false movement
2. Make the opponent react
3. Take advantage of his reaction

Types of feints

1. False movement
2. Eye direction
3. Slow down
4. Change of speed
5. Psychological

Feinting is a delicate balance of physical and psychological deception. It takes a good amount of practice to master. Being able to portray many different ''faces'' in combat gives you an added edge.

DRAWING

Drawing is similar to baiting the hook in fishing. The fish sees only his lunch, not the hook that lies inside. To bait your opponent, intentionally expose a target for him to attack. This can be done by three methods. The first is to assume a vulnerable stance that leaves an opening. Try this in the beginning stages of the fight. Once you have shown your true stance, the opponent is unlikely to believe that it will change. The only exception to this is if you appear tired or hurt.

The second draw is to expose a vital point, such as your head and let the opponent come in for an attack. When he commits to a high attack, evade and respond with a counterattack to his low section. Use this formula for high-low, right-left and back-front attacks.

The final case is to step back and let your opponent step forward. As soon as he begins to step in, go in suddenly like a tidal wave, and overwhelm him. Drawing, like feinting, requires practice and deception to be effective.

SET-UP

Setting-up is often confused with drawing or feinting. While drawing and feinting lure the opponent into your trap, a set-up uses the opponent's strength, habit or preconceived thought against him. The best way to understand a set-up is to look at some examples.

EXAMPLE I

Attack the opponent continuously with a straight punch to the face. He will raise his guard to block, expecting that the punches are your only strategy. When he becomes comfortable with his defense, attack with a hook kick to the leg. Make him create a habit, based on your habit. When you break your habit, he will be unprepared to respond.

EXAMPLE 2

Attack with kicking combinations and give your opponent time to adjust to your kicking style. When he feels confident handling your kicks, rush in and throw him to the ground. Your unexpected change of tactics will catch him off guard.

EXAMPLE 3

If you know the opponent well, you will not have to spend time to create a habit or psychological pattern as in the first two examples. For example, if you know he likes to counter with his right hook kick, give him a short right hook kick to the body. While he is countering with his favorite technique, follow up with a back kick to the groin. This will make him hesitate to use his best skill again soon.

Indirect attacking is a more advanced skill than direct attacking. Most beginners learn direct attacks first and move to indirect attacks at the intermediate or advanced level. Before you try indirect attacking techniques, you must understand the principles of direct attacks. Indirect attacks are based on the anticipation of a direct attack by your opponent. Without knowing what type of direct attack the opponent will use, indirect attacking is not possible.

A set-up uses the opponent's strength, habit or preconceived thought against him.

CHAPTER 6
COMBINATION ATTACKS

When your first attack, whether direct or indirect, fails, follow with a second and third attack. Attack continuously until you achieve your original goal. Combination attacking can be in the form of planned combinations or can evolve as the combat unfolds. Always be prepared with a back-up plan.

Combination attacks are usually direct attacks. You also can begin with an indirect attack and follow up with direct attacks. There are three purposes for using a combination attack:

1. To gain the advantage in the use of space and time
2. To follow up a failed or ineffective attack to avoid losing the prevailing momentum
3. To finish the fight with a variety of attacks topped off by a powerful finishing blow

There are many variations of combination attacks, however there are two basic styles. The combination traditionally supports the main attack, with the main attack either coming first and being followed by the supporting blows or with the supporting blows leading up to the main attack. The supporting blows are used primarily to fill the space that the opponent might use for counterattacking or escaping.

For example, step forward moving both hands in front of your body to simulate wild blocking motions. Close the distance while the opponent is trying to figure out what you are doing and then attack with a takedown. This example has the supporting actions preceding the main action. Or you can go in directly with a hook to the knee as the main attack. If this fails, step in and follow up with an outside takedown to finish.

Junsado categorizes combination attacks into four groups:

Group A: 1. Strike + strike
               2. Strike + kick
               3. Strike + immobilization
               4. Strike + takedown

Group B: 1. Kick + strike
               2. Kick + kick
               3. Kick + immobilization
               4. Kick + takedown

Group C: 1. Immobilization + strike
               2. Immobilization + kick
               3. Immobilization + takedown

Group D: 1. Takedown + strike
               2. Takedown + kick
               3. Takedown + immobilization (pin)

These basic formulas can be compounded in any way that works for you. If you combine Group A #1 and Group B #1, you will come up with a sequence of straight punch, hook punch, hook kick, and knife strike to the neck. If you combine Group B #3 and Group C #3, you will have a complex combination of hook kick to the kidney, grab the   arm and arm lock, reverse the arm lock to an outside wrist lock and force the opponent to the ground. Experiment with the possibilities of compounding the groups.

COMBINATION ATTACKING

Group A #1 plus Group B #1 equals straight punch, hook punch, hook kick, and knife strike.

Advantages of Combinations:

1. You can capitalize on your physical and mental momentum without interruption.
2. You don't have to wait for another opening to appear.
3. The opponent is forced into a defensive posture and you gain the psychological advantage.
4. The opponent is confused, allowing you to control the rhythm of the fight.
5. You can achieve a powerful finish.

Disadvantages of Combinations:

1. You have to be agile and skilled in attacking.
2. An experienced opponent can escape by stepping back or to the side or jam by stepping in.
3. You can easily lose your balance when shifting from one technique to the next.
4. You can lose control of the distance between you and your opponent.
5. You need stamina to attack strongly until the final movement is complete.
6. You become vulnerable to a counter attack.

When you practice continuous attacking, be aware of the drawbacks. Practice moving quickly without hesitation. Study yourself to know how and when to focus and release your internal energy. Learn how to spot openings while you are in motion. Above all, never rush into a continuous attack without a specific goal in mind.

STRATEGY

CHAPTER 7
COMBAT RANGE

Simply put, combat range is the distance between you and your opponent. This is, however, a broad definition and can be interpreted in many ways. To apply combat range to the science of strategy, you will need a more specific working definition. Combat range has to be thought of in two dimensions: real distance and relative distance. First practice real distance skills and when you understand them, look at the implications of relative distance.

REAL DISTANCE

Real distance is the distance from the end of the aggressors longest viable weapon to the nearest part of the defender's body to which that weapon can be applied. If your opponent's longest weapon is a stick and your nearest exposed body part is your front hand, the distance between the end of the stick and your hand will determine the combat range.

However, a stick does not pose as serious a threat to your hand as it does to your head, so you also have to consider the vulnerability of the exposed target. Similarly, there is a high degree of danger when the opponent is in grabbing range of your hand because grabbing presents more of a threat to your hand than striking does. This is where relative distance will begin to blur the lines of real distance.

In real distance, there are four ranges: neutral, long, medium and short.

NEUTRAL RANGE

Definition
Neutral range is the distance at which neither combatant can effectively attack with the weapons available.

Advantages
The neutral range gives you the time to prepare your strategy and ample opportunity to change plans as you observe your opponent. The neutral range is the ideal range from which to begin the confrontation because you can ready yourself immediately.

Disadvantages
The neutral distance leaves you vulnerable to a surprise attack from your opponent because when you are at a neutral distance, your mind is less alert than at any other range. Don't discount the possibility of an attack from any distance. Be prepared at all times.

Neutral distance is inefficient for attacking because an attack that covers a lengthy distance is easy to detect and avoid.

How to attack
Attacks from neutral range require explosive speed and deception. To create speed, use quick footwork and combined movements. Feinting, set-ups and traps are all ways of confusing your opponent to create an opening for a surprise attack.

Tactics
Be alert and study your opponent in the neutral range. Be prepared to counter or reverse a surprise attack. In addition to surprise attacks, you can try to outwait your opponent. Eventually one of you will become impatient and attack. If you are patient, your opponent will attack first and give you the chance for a counter. This tactic requires patience and an iron will.

LONG RANGE

Definition

The long range is the distance at which either combatant can strike easily with their longest attacking implement usually by kicking or by striking or cutting with a weapon.

Advantages

Long range is ideal for kicking or for using a long hand held weapon such as the stick or sword. In long range combat, you can easily protect your vital organs and still strike the opponent in a split second. Long range strikes are good for applying maximum force in every strike because you have enough space to create acceleration force with long, powerful weapons.

Disadvantages

The long range and neutral range have similar disadvantages due to the amount of time a long strike takes to reach its target. It is both slower and more difficult to conceal than a short attack. Long attacks also leave you vulnerable immediately after the attack because you must sacrifice some space and time to execute a long range strike properly. Give special attention to maintaining your guard between long range attacks.

How to attack

Long range combat is well suited to linear and thrusting attacks. Take advantage of the time gap between your attack and your opponent's response by following up every attack with another. Make maximum use of footwork to cover and close the distance between you.

Tactics

Study your opponent's speed and habits. Understand his style so you can adjust your timing accordingly. Use both regular and irregular rhythms to confuse your opponent and draw him into your attack. Attack decisively and follow-up every attack with compound combinations.

MEDIUM RANGE

Definition
Medium range is the distance at which a target can easily be reached with hand attacks including striking, locking, grabbing, pushing and choking.

Advantages
Medium range emphasizes upper body strength and the dexterity of the hands allowing you to grab and strike with pinpoint accuracy. It gives you the opportunity to immobilize your opponent in a single lightning strike. Kicking is another option for medium range, but should be confined to short, powerful kicks to the low and middle targets.

Disadvantages
At the medium range, you can expect to exchange blows and sustain some damage in the course of executing your plan. Your vital points are in range of a serious attack and the possibility of a knockout or deadly strike to the head or body is high.

How to attack
Medium range attacks require you to use the full range of motion of your arms and legs to create circular force. Use the angles of your joints to intensify the force. Grabbing becomes important at the medium range to control the opponent and limit his ability to attack and counter.

Tactics
Mobility and strength in the upper body are assets in medium range combat. Strong attacks and quick evasion will give you the upper hand. Use many diverse attacks and strategies to keep yourself safe and control the distance that is most comfortable for you.

SHORT RANGE

Definition
Short range combat is close fighting or ground fighting in which the combatants are fully engaged including locking, choking, pinning, clinching and other forms of grappling. It is also ideal for short strikes like elbow and knee strikes.

Advantages
Short range combat is filled with surprise attacks and infighting. Because you are so close to your opponent, he will not be able to see your entire body at any one time. Use hidden weapons to attack and demoralize him. Infighting is excellent against anyone who likes to keep you at a distance and work his strategy. Get inside his range and prevent him from attacking effectively.

Disadvantages
Short range fighting requires great strength and endurance because you must actively resist your opponent while executing your strategy. There is a high risk of head, neck, spine and joint injuries as a result of throwing, locking and grappling attacks. Take caution not to fall into your opponents trap or you may find yourself totally immobilized.

How to attack
To attack effectively in short range combat, develop the junsado strategy of the circle and the triangle. Short range attacks are often not clear cut and you must know how to escape and reverse many types of grappling skills. Understand how to attack vital areas, how to create your force frame and how to destroy the opponent's force frame. Develop finishing tactics

Tactics
Ground or close fighting requires strength, endurance and determination. Get a good grip on your opponent. Hold on until you are

COMBAT RANGES

Neutral Range

Long Range

Medium Range

Short Range

able to prevail. Plan your strategy several moves ahead to outwit your opponent.

RELATIVE DISTANCE

Real distance is determined by the absolute measure of distance from one point to another. However, this objective measure will work only in a world where all people are physical and mental equals. Since this is untrue, you cannot rely on real distance alone to determine your combat strategy.

Relative distance is used to account for the many mitigating factors. In addition to considering the actual physical distance, consider these elements in terms of both you and your opponent:

1. Skill level
2. Mental toughness
3. Speed
4. Size
5. Types of available weapons (bodily and other)
6. Vulnerability of targets exposed
7. Type of techniques available

Although the real distance is the same, the relative distance is affected by the size of the partners.

Example 1

In neutral and long range combat, you used speed to initiate an attack. However, if your opponent is faster than you, you will easily be countered before you complete the attack. Similarly, if your opponent has a knife or other edged weapon, your ability to rush in will be limited by the danger of a cutting attack. If your opponent has his vital targets well covered, you will have to spend more time drawing him out before you can use a speedy attack.

Example 2

In medium range combat, an exposed hand or arm is a prime target to grab and use as an initiation point for a joint lock. However, in long range combat, an exposed hand or arm presents little opportunity for a main attack because striking to the hand is not a serious blow. A target that is open for a main attack at one range is only good for an initiation or transitional technique at another.

As you might imagine, this complicates the concept of real distance significantly. In fact, the ability to judge and compensate for relative distance is the mark of a master strategist. Relative distance judgment comes from study, experience and instinct. You can study, practice and perfect real distance with consistent effort, but for relative distance you must experience the added element of unpredictability. No two opponents will act or react the same. Take every opportunity to engage many types of opponents in practice and arranged combat to hone your relative distance judgment.

LENGTHEN YOUR RANGE

The farther away you can execute an initiative attack from, the more likely you are to succeed in combat. By lengthening the distance of your optimum long range attack, you improve your chances to defeat a higher percentage of opponents. If your long range is longer than your opponent's, there will be a distance at which you attack him, but he cannot attack you.

Imagine you can comfortably attack your opponent from five feet. If your opponent's maximum range is four feet, select a distance that is more than four but less than five feet from him. This is the distance from which you can safely prepare and launch your attack without the threat of an initiative attack by your opponent. This is the ultimate goal of range fighting.

Lengthening your range is possible through improving or compensating for four elements of your combat arsenal.

Footwork

If you have excellent footwork, you can position yourself farther away from your opponent and still reach him easily. Quick footwork will allow you to cover a greater distance in a shorter time. If your footwork is not good, develop better timing and the ability to spot openings. Then instead of going to your opponent, wait for him to move and take advantage of the opening created by his movement.

Stride

To improve your footwork, first determine the length of your average step or stride when you move forward and backward. If your stride is long, you will not only be able to cover more distance in each step, you will be able to create more powerful blows. Each step will add momentum and acceleration force to your attacks. If your average step is short, do not try to lengthen it. Taking uncomfortably long steps will leave you vulnerable and unbalanced. Instead, use many short, quick steps to slip in and attack. Short steps are used for deceptive speed attacks and long steps are used for powerful, long distance attacks.

Flexibility

When you face an unknown adversary, he will calculate what he expects your range to be based on what he can see, including your size. However, good flexibility is a hidden weapon. Good flexibility allows your initiative attacks to reach farther than your opponent estimates. By lengthening your range of motion, you will be able to launch surprise attacks from a greater distance than your opponent. If you are not flexible, develop your footwork for a similar effect.

Distance control

There are two ways to control the distance between you and your opponent without risking an initiative attack. Feinting, where you simulate an attack and then change course according to your opponent's response, is a good choice for people with good reflexes and speed. Feinting will confuse your opponent and momentarily disturb his sense of distance. Trick him into assuming you are moving in a certain direction. When he adjusts to your movement, attack. **Range feinting** is deceiving your opponent into committing to a range other than the one of your actual attack. During his adjustment, he will be unable to respond to your change of tactics.

For example, you and your opponent are in a neutral range stand-off with neither person willing to commit to an initiative attack. Take a quick step backward. To adjust to your movement and maintain his neutral range, your opponent will take one step forward. As soon as he begins to step, take a quick step forward and launch a decisive attack. You have deceived him by changing what he thought would be a neutral range into long range.

The second method of distance control is drawing. **Drawing** means intentionally leaving an open target for your opponent to attack. When he confidently comes in to attack, counter with a short, unexpected blow. Feinting and drawing can help you compensate if you are unable to quickly or confidently close the distance between you and your opponent. By making your opponent come to you, you conserve energy and lessen the risk of a counterattack.

To summarize, the more you can lengthen your range, the better chance you have of winning. However, if you cannot improve your range, compensate by developing footwork, feinting, and drawing skills.

SUMMARY OF RANGE FIGHTING

In combat, the outcome favors the participant who makes the bets use of the space and time allotted. In terms of space, which we have discussed as distance or range, there are three choices:

1. **Use the given space to attack.**
2. **Transform the space to your advantage.**
3. **Create space to attack.**

Using the space you have is the best method. Making your opponent move and then using the transformed space is the second best case. Creating space in which to attack is reserved as a last resort because of the skillful initiation necessary to produce an attacking opportunity.

CHAPTER 8
CIRCLE AND TRIANGLE

Change is the primary characteristic of every living being. When change ceases to occur, life ends. There is not a single living thing on Earth that is not in a constant state of change. Some changes are not readily evident because they occur slowly at the molecular level, but they exist just the same.

Change is also characteristic of activities and events perpetuated by living beings. Combat, which always needs living participants to exist, is subject to constant, rapid changes. Whether it is a personal confrontation that lasts only seconds or a world war that lasts for years, combat requires adaptation and adjustment to changes.

In essence, there are three ways to react to the changes of combat. The most desirable reaction is to **create the changes**. This is an offensive posture. By creating change, you become a dynamic force and direct the outcome of the confrontation. The second option is to **react to the changes** created by your adversary or the environment. This is a defensive posture. Action is always preferable to reaction, so a defensive attitude should be assumed only when the changes are too great for you to control.

If you fail to create or react to the changes, you will become their victim. If you stand idly by as your opponent dictates the direction of the encounter, you will lose every time. This is true in combat and this is true in life. Successful people create change or at least manage it.

Change is effected in many ways, but there are two elements of change that must be considered foremost: changes in time and changes in space. Time moves on with or without us. The march of time existed long before we were born and will go on long after we have died. There is no known way to stop the passing of time. To cope with changes in time, adaptation is necessary. Short of being able to stop or turn back time, we can make wise use of the time we have.

The ability to gauge time, known as timing, is a major aspect of combat. When to move, how fast to move, when not to move, when to make your opponent move, how fast your opponent moves - these are all changes confined by time. If you miss the chance to attack or you move too slowly, the chance is over and you can never recover it.

The second determinant of change is space. Space can be described in several ways - the space between you and your opponent, the space you occupy with your body, and the space available for attacking and maneuvering. Each type of space affects the changes that take place in the course of an encounter.

Space, unlike time, can be manipulated to give the appearance of being created or destroyed. The space available actually remains the same, but its appearance is transformed by you. For example, if you take one step forward toward your opponent, you appear to have destroyed some space in which your opponent can attack or maneuver. However, what you have really done is caused the space to appear differently to your opponent. He can then create another change by stepping back or he can react to your change by counterattacking in the new space.

There are many ways of using space and time to create changes to your advantage. By feinting, drawing, faking, and using deceptive footwork, you take control of or distort your opponent's concept of space. Similarly by using a combination of regular and irregular rhythm, multiple attacks, faking, and footwork, you can break your opponent's normal judgment of time.

These tactics are commonly used and practiced by many people. To win over a skilled combat practitioner, however, an additional edge is necessary. Junsado goes beyond conventional combat theory with the principles of the circle and the triangle and their application to controlling time and space in combat.

THE CIRCLE

The circle is the single most prominent symbol in the combat arts. It has been used for thousands of years to express infinity, harmony, serenity and wisdom. But these are only the most commonly designated meanings. Is it possible that some warriors found other, unrevealed meanings in the circle? Perhaps as you study the uses of the circle in junsado, you will find the hidden meanings of the infamous circle.

OFFENSIVE GOALS

There are three goals that can be accomplished through circular motion:

To adjust to the opponent's initiative attack

By moving in a circle with your opponent, you lessen the force of his attack. If the opponent pulls your left shoulder to the left with his right hand, move your left foot to the left following his pulling force and pull his left shoulder to the right with your right hand. Both of you will be moving in a circle with at least similar force, allowing you to maintain your balance and prepare a response. Going with the attacker instead of resisting, reduces or neutralizes the amount of energy expended and gives you the chance not only to react to the change, but to take the advantageous position of creating change by setting up a takedown with your movement.

To counterattack

Circular movement is ideal for counterattacking. When countering, the goal is to hit the opponent where he is open, usually an opening created by his attacking posture. If you are attacked by a high punch, counter with a low kick. If you are attacked by a right leg hook kick, counter with a right leg hook kick. If you are attacked by a left leg hook kick, counter with a left leg hook kick.

If you try these combinations with a partner, you will see that when attacking with the left side, the right side is open. When attacking high, a low target is open. This is a natural phenomenon that occurs when the attacker disturbs his defensive equilibrium to attack. You cannot attack and maintain perfect defense at the same time. There is always a complementary opening, no matter how briefly.

A circular counter attack

To destroy the opponent's balance.
Circular movement is excellent for destroying the opponent's balance. Circular movements create two opposing but complementary forces that follow each other on the circumference of the circle. Examples include hip throws, shoulder throws and rear hook takedowns.

The theory of the circle applies to many different movements. The primary circles found in combat are:

1. The circle created by the movement of you and your opponent moving together.
2. The circle created by one person moving independently of the other.
3. The circle created by the movement of individual body parts.
4. The circle created by the force of one or a series of movements or blows.
5. The circle created by one person's manipulation of the other.

Circular motion has the added advantage of centripetal force, a naturally occurring phenomenon that has been used for centuries to aid the weak in defeating the strong. When you move your arms and legs in circular kicking or striking motions, you become the center of the circle and the force of your blows is increased by the centripetal force generated. When you execute a throw, your body becomes the center of the circle and initiates the force of the throw. The weight of the opponent increases the centripetal force, which culminates in the impact with the ground.

DEFENSIVE APPLICATIONS

Beyond the general applications covered so far, there are four specific defensive applications of the circle.

Against pinning on the ground

Being pinned on the ground is one of the most difficult situations from which to escape. The aggressor has the advantage of using gravity and his body weight to hold you down. Often your arms and legs are immobilized making striking is impossible. When your arms or legs are pinned, the best method of escape is to take away the opponent's balance.

To break a pin on the ground, line up your opponent's force on one line to take away his balance

The simplest way to break his hold is by moving your upper and lower body from side to side (toward each other) in a rapid, jerking motion. When your opponent moves to adjust his balance, create a triangle force frame (see next section) and topple him off.

A second option is available when both of your hands are pinned on the ground by the attacker's hands. When your attacker exerts force on your hands, move both of your hands quickly in an arc to one side of your body. The force being applied by the attacker will be thrown to one side allowing you again to set up your triangle force frame and escape.

The key to breaking any pinning attack is to line up your opponent's force on a straight line. When he has a wide base of force, he can use his leverage against you. When you make his base shrink, he will have a more difficult time holding you. Ultimately, your goal is to make your base larger than his and throw him off. This concept will be covered in more depth in the triangle principle.

Against any head lock or rear choke

When you are choked or put in a headlock from the side, your opponent's forearm and hand will be in front of your neck. To break this kind of lock, grab your opponent's wrist and elbow and fix them tightly against your body. Then roll over the opponent's forearm and move your head out of the lock by twisting the arm. When you complete your roll, you will have reversed the hold into an arm or wrist lock against the opponent. It is important to hold the elbow and wrist tightly to prevent any resistance by the opponent. The locked arm will be in the shape of a ''Z'' at the end of the technique.

 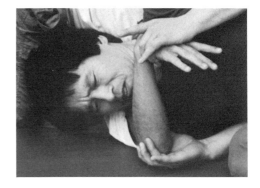

**Reverse a rear choke by rolling over the choking arm
and locking it into a Z shape**

Against any hold or lock

There are two methods of using the circle principle to break a hold or lock. The first is by making yourself the center of the circle and making your opponent move around you. In this case, your feet are stationary or act as a pivot and your upper body is used to control the opponent's direction. (see Fig. 3.5) For example, when grabbed by the shoulder, grab the assailant's hand and press his elbow with your other hand to create an arm bar. Without moving your feet, spin him down to the ground creating a circle with his movement.

Fig. 3.5

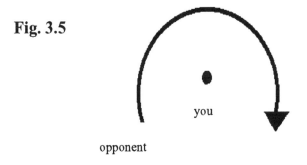

you

opponent

The second method is to make a small circle with your body while causing your opponent to make a larger circle. Here, you may take one or two steps as you direct his movement. (see Fig. 3.6) Using the arm bar example, move your feet several steps rather than remaining stationary as above. By moving, you create more momentum and cover a wider area. This causes the opponent's circle to become larger and the force applied to him is greater.

Fig. 3.6

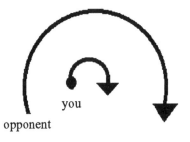

you

opponent

Uncoiling

The final example of the defensive circle is the principle of uncoiling the opponent's lock. Often, a lock entails, twisting one or more limbs to prevent them from moving. To escape from this type of lock, Move the rest of your body in the same twisting direction as the limb has been twisted. An easy example is a cross leg lock in which you are pinned on your stomach and your attacker has both legs folded at the knee with the right leg crossed on top of the left. To escape, uncoil your body to the right by turning over. Your turning motion will uncoil the lock. Always uncoil in the same direction as the force is being applied. If you try to turn to your left in this example, you are unable to move because you are moving against the force.

As you can see, the principle of the circle is broad and complex. Many strategists and martial artists have dedicated their entire lives to studying the applications of the circle in combat. Yet few have revealed their discoveries.

Carefully study the techniques and skills you have learned in both junsado and in other arts thus far. You will find that many of them follow one or more of the principles of the circle. If you are having difficulty working out a technique, especially a grappling skill, try applying one of the circle methods. The circle is one of the most effective weapons in combat strategy. However, the circle has a very strong opposing force - the triangle.

THE TRIANGLE

The circle principle is well known among martial artists and combat strategists. It has many applications and has been studied in depth. The triangle principle on the other hand has remained something of a secret. Perhaps you have never heard of the triangle principle at all.

The triangle is establishes a force frame. A force frame is a structural positioning of your body used to create leverage. It is similar to the steel beams that make up the inner structure of a tall building. Without a well designed inner structure the building will collapse. The same is true in combat.

For offense, the triangle is useful in ground fighting. By creating a triangle with any three points on your body you can pin and hold your opponent firmly on the ground. For example, if you sit on your opponent's chest and pin both of his arms with your hands, you have created a triangle with your right hand, left hand and lower body as the three points. Similarly, in standing combat, you can create a triangle by planting your two feet squarely apart and gripping the opponent with your hands, such as a rear choke hold.

In each of these cases, you set up a triangle shaped force frame with your weight on the most stable point or points and force being applied by the remaining point(s). On the ground, your lower body bears the weight and your hands apply the force. If you put your weight on your hands, you become susceptible to a counter by the circle. In the standing example, your feet bear the weight and your arm applies the force to the opponent's neck.

The offensive triangle is a combination of base (weight bearing points) and force application. With a stable base and a strong force application, the triangle is an unbeatable offense.

The triangle is also applicable to defense in ground fighting by establishing a force frame in your favor. If you are pinned in a prone position, the most efficient method of escaping is the triangle, because it does not require the use of your hands or arms.

In almost every ground attack, your arms are immobilized first. When this happens, use your body to form a triangle on the ground with your knees and shoulders as the points. For example, if your are pinned on your stomach, draw one knee up under your body and align the other side of your body on one line. Topple the opponent off by using your aligned shoulder and both knees as leverage points.

When pinned, create a triangle force frame to escape

The aligned side of your body creates the base of the triangle which bears your weight. Your bent knee creates space in which to move and breaks the opponent's triangle by lifting one of his base points off the ground. When you have established the triangle shape, explosively push upward with your bent knee and roll your body to the side that is aligned. Your opponent will be toppled off and you will have the opportunity to regain control of the confrontation.

CIRCLE VS. TRIANGLE

Thus far, you have learned ways both to create and destroy the force of the circle and the triangle. The triangle and circle are, in fact, opposing forces. While you can use a circle to defeat a circle and a triangle to defeat a triangle, it is far more effective to use one against the other. Look at the following examples.

1. **Circle defeats circle** - the attacker attempts an inside sweep (●) of the defender's foot. The defender grabs the attacker and counters with a sacrifice throw (●).

2. **Circle defeats triangle** - The attacker applies a choke hold from behind (▲) on the ground. The defender grabs the attacker's arm and rolls forward (●) as in circular defensive application two (p. 142) to convert the choke into an elbow/wrist lock.

3. **Triangle defeats triangle** - The attacker pins the defender face down on the ground by sitting on his back and holding both arms down (▲). The defender draws his knee up (▲) and uses the resulting leverage to topple the attacker off him.

4. **Triangle defeats circle** - The attacker attempts a hip throw (●). The defender lowers his center of gravity and uses his hand to apply downward force to the attacker's hips setting up a triangle force frame.

The surprise element of using the circle against the triangle and the triangle against the circle gives you an advantage in combat. Study both principles as they apply to your style of combat and as they apply to combat in general. If there is a weakness in what you are doing, use the circle or triangle to strengthen it. If the circle or triangle dominates in your art, study how it can be countered by the opposing principle. Know the strength of your art and the weaknesses within the strength. Never assume any strength is perfect. The irony of a strong point is that if you rely on it heavily, it becomes a weakness.

CHAPTER 9

ATTRIBUTES

Strategic theory is a guide to combat you will ever encounter. It attempts to find workable solutions to the changes that occur during combat. It fails, however, to account for the living element of combat, the human element.

If people were perfect beings, with everyone being equal in all ways, strategy would direct the outcome of every confrontation and the results would be predictable according to the strategic positions adopted by both sides.

The nature of combat is such that equals rarely meet. Combat occurs between humans who are a delicate balance of various weak and strong attributes. The combination of these attributes with the level of physical skill and strategic instinct of the combatants determines the ultimate victor in any contest.

The central attributes of combat, from one-on-one to full scale war, are:

1. Timing
2. Rhythm
3. Speed
4. Accuracy
5. Power
6. Coordination
7. Stamina

TIMING

Timing is the ability to control the speed of your attack so it reaches its maximum efficiency at the proper moment. Timing is a combination of speed, accuracy and reflexes. To achieve proper timing, you must synchronize the various parts of your body to fit the speed of the movement being executed.

There are two types of timing: action timing and reaction timing. **Action timing** means selecting the right action at the right time. Simply put, find an opening and take advantage of it. Action timing is used for initiative attacks against a neutral or defensive opponent.

Reaction timing is assessing your opponent's offensive movements and selecting a proper response. It is commonly used in counterattacking. Reaction timing is always in response to an attack by the opponent and is more difficult to establish than action timing.

Both types of timing require good perception and judgment, accurate muscular response and correct performance of the intended movement. The body and brain must be synchronized to assess the current situation, select a proper response and execute the response in the time allowed.

There are several formulas you can use to hone your reaction timing.

1. Attack when the opponent is preparing his attack. His mind is occupied with what to do next and he is not fully prepared to attack or defend.
2. Attack when the opponent steps forward or backward. The key is to attack before his stepping foot touches the ground. While one foot is in the air, the balance of the body is easily upset, but once the step is completed, an attack is imminent.
3. Attack when the opponent's attack is at its maximum height. He is unable to retreat quickly and his balance is extremely vulnerable when his body is fully extended.
4. Attack when the opponent hesitates or is nervous. His indecision is your cue that he has mentally let down his guard and is vulnerable to attack.

Attack when the opponent's attack is at is maximum height

5. Attack just after your opponent completes an attacking movement. Every muscle needs a brief period of recovery between exertions. Take advantage of this by attacking as soon as the movement is finished.

6. Attack when your opponent changes stance or position. He is committed to finishing the change and temporarily unable to respond.

7. Attack when your opponent is tired or careless. His mental fatigue is an indication that he does not have the stamina to respond strongly to your attack.

RHYTHM

Rhythm and timing are often used interchangeably by novice fighters. Timing is a specific action that takes place at a specific point in time. Rhythm, on the other hand, is a sustained pattern of actions over a period of time.

Rhythm is established by creating a pattern of regular and irregular movements through a combination of strong and weak pulses. Normally, the rhythm of attacking is strong and the rhythm of withdrawing is weak. By checking the attacking and withdrawing pattern of your opponent, you can determine his rhythm. He will use a similar method to find your rhythm.

To confuse his perception of your rhythm, practice attacking very aggressively, like a hurricane. Before he realizes your intention to attack, initiate without hesitation. Then withdraw like a squirrel, fast and strong with only the goal of retreating in mind. This will prevent him from finding a pattern of weak and strong beats. When you have established a strong/strong pattern, occasionally use a strong/weak sequence to create an irregular pattern in your attacks.

Sensing the opponent's ability to make or break the weak/strong pattern is very important in establishing the rhythm of the confrontation. When you disrupt your opponent's weak/strong pattern and make your rhythm the rhythm of the fight, you will dominate. This is sometimes called ''ring generalship'' in boxing. When you have the dominating rhythm, speed becomes secondary and you can attack at will without hesitation.

SPEED

Speed is the rate in time at which your movement travels. Speed in junsado strategy refers to quickness of mind, quickness of perception, and quickness of physical movements. Generally, speed training focuses on the ability to move the body or parts of the body quickly.

This leaves out a very important part of speed, which is the ability to perceive and assess the given situation and formulate a response rapidly. Perception and response are the root from which physical speed grows. Without knowing that a response is demanded, the body will never create a speedy movement. Cultivate mental speed by always being aware of your surroundings and by understanding the possible outcomes of the situation.

Develop physical speed through constant training. Physical speed is enhanced by muscle strength, muscle elasticity, and the capacity of the muscle to respond explosively. To build muscle strength for speed, concentrate on exercises that make the muscles stronger while maintaining flexibility. Any exercise that causes the muscle to shorten or tighten, such as heavy lifting, will have an adverse affect on speed training. To prevent the muscles from tightening up because of strength training, stretch regularly before and after your workouts. Stretching will keep the muscles long and supple, enabling them to move more freely.

Finally, develop explosive speed by repeatedly exposing the muscles to circumstances in which they must respond explosively. Muscles are made up of slow twitch fibers and fast twitch fibers. The fast twitch fibers control the explosive reactions necessary to create speed, so these are the fibers you want to increase. The only way to increase the fast twitch fibers is to create demand in the muscle.

Exercises that require the muscle to produce speed while moving against resistance are excellent for increasing fast twitch fibers. These exercises include interval training, uphill running, explosive weight training, and training with wrist and ankle weights. Be cautious when training for speed with resistance, because excess stress on the muscle is transferred to the ligaments and joints which are very susceptible to stress injuries.

In addition to the explosive speed of single movements, there is transitional speed, which is the quickness with which you move from

Keys to Speed

Perception
Response time
Muscle strength
Muscle elasticity
Explosive initiation
Transitional speed

one movement to the next. Transitional speed comes from economy of motion and moving according to the mechanics of your body. Awkward, overly powerful or overextended movements will reduce your transitional speed because of the compensation required. Having to compensate for poorly executed techniques wastes time and energy. Once you finish your intended movement, there should be little to no extra energy expended until you begin your next movement.

ACCURACY

Accuracy is precision in movement. In combat, precision is measured by the result of the movement. If the movement reaches its target or performs its proper function, it is considered accurate. In accuracy, absolute perfection is required. An almost accurate movement and an accurate movement produce entirely different results.

If you successfully block a kick, your block was accurate. If you almost block the kick but get hit, your block was inaccurate. There cannot be a middle ground in accuracy.

To improve your accuracy, practice every movement with an intentional effort to focus the technique onto a specific target. Never practice randomly. Before you practice any movement, think about the goal of the movement. Plan how to execute and what target to aim for. When you practice with focus, your free combat will require less thought because you have already considered the function of every movement.

Accuracy also requires a good sense of distance. When you apply force to another body, you must first calculate the proper distance for striking. If the distance is too long, you will not reach the target or the strike will lack power. If the distance is too short, you will not be able to extend the strike fully and it will be cut short by your opponent. To strike accurately, create a distance that will allow you to strike with penetration and still finish the technique fully.

POWER

Power is force exerted over time. In terms of physical movements that translates into physical strength and speed. The more physical strength and speed you have, the more power you can produce.

Speed and strength are not equal partners in building power. An increase in speed will have more effect than an increase in strength. However, speed is more difficult than strength to increase quantitatively. Strength can be increased by overloading the individual or groups of muscles until they grow in size to meet the demand.

Strength training for combat should develop long supple muscles like those of dancers, swimmers and gymnasts. To develop muscles without inhibiting speed, use many reps with small, consistent overloads. Concentrate on weight training rather than weight lifting.

To maximize your power, develop a suitable balance of speed and strength. If you rely heavily on speed, you will be fast, but your impact will be minimal. If you rely heavily on strength your movements will be slow and heavy, preventing them from reaching the target before it disappears.

COORDINATION

Coordination is the harmonious balance of all of your bodily parts, including your brain. Total body coordination is something that comes naturally to some people. They are called natural athletes. Most people, however, must work hard at developing total body coordination.

To improve coordination takes practice and an understanding of the mechanics of the human body. Poorly coordinated people are those who work against the natural design of their body. Slow practice is best to begin learning a new movement. Concentrate on the path of the movement and the muscles used, until you can execute comfortably.

Once you have a rough imitation of the technique, begin to increase your speed smoothly and gradually. Build up to maximum speed only when you make consistently good repetitions at normal speed. When your technique is fluid in individual practice, begin to apply the movement in realistic situations such as free combat and sparring. Do not to move up to full speed until your applications are fluid and natural.

Besides skill related training, you can practice coordination drills like rope jumping and spatial relations exercises like tumbling, flipping, and jumping toe touches to improve the communication between your brain and body.

For some people, coordination is very difficult to build, but it comes to everyone eventually. Slow deliberate practice and perseverance will bring results.

STAMINA

Stamina is the fortitude of mental and physical character to endure or overcome fatigue.

Stamina consists primarily of the physical ability to endure prolonged stress. Stress can be performing a demanding activity over a period of time or being physically injured. In combat, both are likely to occur if the fight continues long enough. To increase your ability to endure a long period of difficult activity, develop your heart/lung capacity. Regularly engage in activities that require endurance like distance running, biking, skiing, swimming, long workouts, shadow or partner sparring.

To increase your capacity to endure the stress of being hit and hurt, know how to manage your mind. To withstand an attack, try to remove any negative emotion you have regarding the attacker. Next, set a specific goal to reach and focus on reality rather than illusions. For example, decide that you will withstand the attack until you can escape or that you will take the first opening you spot and overwhelm the attacker until he withdraws. With a specific goal in mind, you can busy yourself with the steps to accomplish that goal. This will take your mind off the physical unpleasantness psychological uncertainty you are experiencing.

In addition to these attributes, there are several intangible characteristics that can affect the outcome when the traditional attributes of each side are evenly matched. These characteristics will be covered in "Section Four: Beyond Tactics".

BOOK   FOUR

BEYOND   TACTICS

CHAPTER 1
BEYOND TACTICS

Strategy and tactics can be confining or can give you total freedom in combat.

When you begin training, you feel free because the tactics and strategy allow you to handle situations that were previously unmanageable. As you practice and use each skill, it becomes familiar and you begin to take it for granted. Soon, you come to depend on the skill because it is easy to use. Eventually, you become confined by the skill itself. This is the natural process of learning.

To master a skill, however, it is necessary to go one step beyond the basic learning process. Let's look at an example. When you begin learning free combat, you often get hit by hook kicks to the stomach. To avoid getting kicked, you learn to use a low section block. This works well and you practice it until you are quite good at it. Soon, whenever you see a middle section hook kick coming, you automatically block it with a low section block.

Then, one day, you try your trusty low section block on a different opponent only to find that he follows every hook kick with a strike to your head. No matter how well you use the low section block, you still get hit by the second attack. Now you are confined by that technique.

To break out of the confinement, rethink your conditioned response. There are many possible counters to a hook kick. Practice side stepping with a counter hook kick or back stepping with a back kick. When you begin to add these skills, you will experience the same cycle of freedom and confinement until one day, without warning, you will go beyond the tactics of defending against hook kick.

You will naturally be able to respond to a hook kick attack without any conscious thought of which counterattack to use. You may use a low block or a hook kick or a back kick or something else entirely, but it will be without hesitation. It will be a free expression of your skill.

In the early stages of training, this may not happen at all. As you become more experienced and skilled, you will begin to see small instances of this, but they will be rare. Mastery comes in small steps that are so gradual that they often may be unrecognizable. As you approach mastery, your experiences of spontaneous perfection will increase in number and frequency.

Mastery of a particular tactic means that it is so natural no one can recognize it as a tactic. Your attacking is so explosive your opponent does not recognize the attack until it is too late to respond. Your feinting is so deceptive your opponent is unable to recognize it as a feint and commits totally to a response to your feint. Your blocking blends in perfectly with your attacking. Your attacking motion is so fast and deceptive that the opponent cannot formulate a reaction until he has already been hit.

The result of mastery is absolute, unchangeable success. It comes like the changing of the seasons. As summer changes to autumn, the days vary between warm and cool. Slowly, naturally, the transformation takes place. By the time you realize that the cold late autumn weather has arrived, winter is already beginning to set in.

To master the tactics of combat, go beyond the conscious act of the tactic itself. When you no longer need the tactic, you have mastered it.

TRANSCENDENTAL TACTICS

The junsado theory of ''beyond tactics'' categorizes three methods for transcending the confinement of individual tactics and skills. The first method is **Transcendental Tactics**. Transcendental refers to the ability to adapt to the given situation without being confined by a single predetermined response. Your response is not tied to rules or precepts.

In combat, a novice assumes his best stance from the beginning of the confrontation. The experienced fighter, however, conceals his tactics from the opponent. He is able to apply power, effort and technical excellence from any stance or position. He is prepared to move in any direction, at any angle, any time. He has transcended the tactic of the "fighting stance" by making any stance his fighting stance.

Mastery of the stance makes it impossible for the opponent to gauge the experience of the fighter. The stance appears weak, but is strong. If the opponent is attached to the conventional concept of a fighting stance, he may think the fighter is inexperienced and drop his guard accordingly.

To transcend a tactic like the fighting stance, you must fully understand the conventional tactic and master it. Only then can you transfer the inherent qualities of the conventional tactic into other types of unconventional tactics. Simply skipping over the conventional tactic works occasionally, but leaves you vulnerable to those fighters who understand the nature of both conventional and unconventional tactics.

CHANGE OF TACTICS

Change of tactics states that if conventional tactics work, use them and if not abandon them for what works. Use every available option until you succeed. There are situations where even the mastery of conventional tactics is not enough to save you.

If you try striking and it fails, change to grabbing or throwing. If that doesn't work, try locking or immobilization. If that doesn't work, go back to striking. Often a combination of different attacks and tactics can extricate you where a single type of attack cannot. Consequently, junsado emphasizes a diverse array of simple, practical skills that can be combined to defeat any style of opponent.

Often, empty hand striking alone will not be strong enough to defeat your opponent. When you find yourself in this situation, search out and use common environmental weapons. The list of possible environmental weapons is limited only by your creativity. Use whatever is necessary and works for you.

TRANSFORMATION OF TACTICS

Though you master many tactics, you will eventually encounter an opponent who is able to counter your skills with ease. This occasionally happens when you plan to fight a certain type of opponent according to conventional wisdom. If you fight a taller opponent, conventional strategy dictates that you use a guerrilla tactic of hit and run.

Many tall fighters have already become acquainted with this type of strategy and know how to deal with it effectively. If this is the case, transform your hit and run to a different tactic like hit and push. Instead of darting in and retreating, rush in and attack, attack, attack until you push the opponent as far as you can. The ideal goal is to finish the fight before he realizes what is happening.

An alternative way of defeating a tall or countering style opponent is by psyching him out. If he expects you to hit and run, he will be waiting for your initiative attack. Instead of playing into his plan, simply wait. Wait until he becomes impatient enough to initiate and counterattack when you see an opening.

When both you and the opponent are thinking in the same mode, neither of you will move first. If both of you are excellent at infighting or distance fighting or grappling, you will be drawn into a stalemate. When both of you are skilled at defending against your style, victory comes at a high cost. In this circumstance, the first person to successfully switch to a different strategy will be the victor. If your opponent is trying a grappling strategy, cut in or kick him. If he is countering, ambush him. Do what he does not expect from a fighter of your style.

If you try an attack strategy that does not work, change to a different course of action immediately. If the opponent senses that a particular strategy has an exploitable weakness, he will plot his counterattack and wait for you to use it again. You will rarely get away with using the same flawed strategy twice in one fight. Avoid exposing your weaknesses, and when you do, transform your tactics to conceal them.

Every situation can be transformed to your advantage, if you use your most important weapon of all, your brain.

In deploying strategy, conceal it deeply inside you. In the use of strategy, constantly change, transform and transcend it. A good strategy is one that is only detected after the opponent has been destroyed by it.

CHAPTER 2
PSYCHING UP FOR COMBAT

To overcome the surprises and adversities of combat, mental preparation and rehearsal are prerequisites. Psyching-up, the development of an indomitable mental attitude, is a necessity for success in combat.

The ability to psych yourself up is predicated on certain personal qualities including determination, discipline, self-reliance/confidence, commitment to your goals, intrinsic motivation and an optimistic point of view.

DAILY TRAINING

If you train well every day, you will feel more confident when the time comes to perform. Put one hundred percent effort into every training session and work toward specific objectives. Do not train for the sake of training itself. Before every practice session, create a training plan.

Specify your objectives for the day and how you intend to reach them. Based on this outline, plan specific exercises and drills in the amount and with the intensity necessary to accomplish your daily objectives. Approach training with the same mental and physical attitude as you would in real combat. You cannot take a relaxed approach to training and decide to turn on the intensity only for combat. Cultivate intensity in your every action.

Daily objectives are based on long term goals. Take time at least once a week to assess how you are progressing toward your long term goals. If you see a problem with the overall course of your training, make a conscious effort to correct it immediately. Every goal is accomplished through a series of very small actions. Stick to your daily plans and revise them when necessary.

It is almost impossible to say "I'm going to psych-up now" and do it. Your body and brain need familiar cues to indicate that physical and mental arousal is about to occur. To facilitate psyching-up on demand, create a simple routine of arousal cues to perform before every practice or combat session.

Cues are actions that send subconscious messages to the other parts of the body. Consider the elaborate routines that baseball pitchers and hitters go through before they wind up or step up to the plate. These actions make them feel comfortable and help them focus on their performance.

Some suggestions for developing cues are:

1. Self-talk
    Ex: "I can do it", "I'm ready", "I'm the best"
2. Relaxation exercises
    Ex: Stretching, deep breathing, meditation
3. Motivational aids
    Ex: Music, poetry, inspiring quote or anecdote
4. Repetitive exercise
    Ex: Running, jumping rope, bouncing in place
5. Visualization
    Ex: See yourself performing perfectly

Whatever cues you select, practice them routinely before every practice session and feel the power and confidence they give you. Learn to create your own mental space in any surrounding.

COMBAT ASSIMILATION

Beyond technical, tactical and strategic training, combat training requires combat assimilation practice. In assimilation practice, replicate as closely as possible the conditions under which combat might take place. If your training is for competition, secure the necessary equipment and people to help you create a competition-type atmosphere. If you train for spontaneous combat, such as self-protection, try to estimate the climate of such combat and recreate it within reason.

Safety is the only limitation on what is practiced in assimilation training. If your anticipated combat is full contact, practice full contact fighting within the confines of safety rules and equipment. For full contact fighting, prepare yourself to deal with the pain and fatigue you will experience. Both fatigue and pain can cause unexpected reactions if you are not familiar with them. Practice training through similar levels of discomfort to prepare.

When you practice assimilation drills, fight with the same mental and physical disposition you would in a real confrontation. Practice reaching and maintaining your focus under pressure. If you feel comfortable with assimilation training, move to over-assimilation training.

In over-assimilation, the realities of combat are exaggerated to make training more challenging. Fight against bigger, stronger, and more experienced opponents. Train with weights or other physical impediments to your movement. Give yourself disadvantages such as using only one type of skill or bodily weapon. Over-assimilation uses anything that exceeds the normal stresses of combat.

PRECOMBAT PLAN

Before every confrontation, there is a period of waiting. In competition, the period can be hours or days. In self-protection it may be only minutes or seconds. Your ability to control your arousal level in this period will determine how you approach the confrontation.

Many physiological changes are controlled by psychological cues. Negative thoughts cause negative actions. By controlling yourself mentally, you can perform better.

Before combat, focus on positive feelings of power, skill, speed, control, confidence in your training, past successes, and your winning strategy.   Avoid self-doubt and negativism.   Forget the situational factors over which you have no control. Prepare to mobilize your energy quickly and use the psyching-up cues that you rehearsed in training. Assess the level at which you must perform to be successful and visualize it happening without a flaw.

RELAXATION

If your mental state becomes too active before combat, or if you have difficulty returning from your psyched-up state of mind after combat, relaxation techniques can be helpful.   Like psyching-up, relaxation has to be practiced and can be induced through cues.

A simple way to learn relaxation is through progressive muscle relaxation. Begin by tensing a muscle group and then relax it. Work through all of the major muscle groups in each session.   Eventually progress to relaxing the muscles without prior tension.   Increase the number of muscle groups you are consciously able to relax at once.

The next step is to transfer your relaxation skills to your practice sessions.   Concentrate on relaxing your muscles in the pre-movement stage.   Initiate every movement from a relaxed state to increase speed and power.   When you can initiate from a relaxed posture, focus on maintaining that relaxation in all of your nontarget muscles (those not directly used in creating the movement). Finally, try to relax your target muscles until just before the point of impact. This will create maximum speed and improve your endurance by conserving energy.

Practicing relaxation in the comforts of your home or training area will not necessarily help you relax under stress. To enhance your ability to relax under stress, create unfavorable conditions under which to practice your relaxation techniques.   Try to manage your anxiety through relaxation techniques when you feel most stressed, whether in training or in other areas of your life. Constant practice will lead you to success.

MENTAL CONDITIONING

The final key to psyching up effectively is mental conditioning. In combat, there is little time to prepare for what might happen. You must be able to reach your optimum level of intensity any time. This is beyond just psyching-up. Instant intensity comes from consistent daily training. To improve your mental condition:

1. Practice every skill and movement with full intensity.
2. Make each repetition better than the previous.
3. Follow your plan with consistency and determination.
4. Live life with the same alertness you fight with.

Maintaining your peak intensity throughout a bout is the result of conditioning plus endurance. If you get distracted by pain, fear, your opponent, your environment, or other external factors, mental conditioning will help you to refocus on your original goal. Without a strong mind, your focus can easily be distracted by nonessential external factors. **Mental conditioning** helps you to psych-up quickly and improves your mental endurance.

In a match of two equally skilled opponents, the one with greater mental endurance will prevail. Mental endurance allows you to be persistent and reach your goal, despite the blocks your opponent puts in your way.

Mental endurance will give you an aura of toughness and aggressiveness that is intimidating to opponents. There is no opponent more frightening than the one who attacks consistently, no matter what you do. He is impervious to your attacks and seems determined to fight until he prevails. This is the result of strong mental endurance.

Mental conditioning is related to the toughness of the fight and mental endurance is related to the length of the bout. With a combination of both conditioning and endurance, you will develop a determined, indomitable warrior spirit. Warrior spirit gives you the guts to attack, the patience to wait for a better opportunity, and the persistence to finish the fight though you are exhausted. Among the most highly skilled combatants, warrior spirit is all that separates the winners from the losers.

Chapter 3
Emotion in Combat

Emotion shadows every fighter. Some use it to power themselves to victory. Others are defeated by it. No one can honestly say that emotion does not affect the outcome of a conflict between two human beings.

To use the emotion of combat to your advantage, don't avoid it. Try to understand what emotions combat brings out in you and how you can best use them to your advantage. Harnessing and applying your emotions is better than avoiding or denying them.

The most common feelings before and during combat are fear, nervousness and anger.

Fear

Fear has many sources. The most obvious source of fear in any contact activity is **fear of injury**. Before you engage the opponent, you will mentally size him up and consider how much damage he might be able to inflict on you. This mental damage assessment comes from a basic instinct to remain safe.

When you find yourself doing this, reverse your thinking. Think instead about how you have trained to avoid being hit and injured. Focus on the strength of your defense. Visualize how you will easily defend every attack your opponent attempts.

Before you experience being hit, you have an unreasonable amount of fear. By integrating contact training into your workouts, you become comfortable with being hit and anticipate the effects of blows on certain areas of the body. Once you get hit a few times, your fear diminishes. You become used to the sensation of contact.

Practice recovering quickly from contact blows in your training. The human body is equipped with a front line defense system that is activated every time you face a potential physical threat. If you are injured, your body has a short-term coping system that suppresses pain and protects the injury until you are able to escape from danger. Minor injuries are almost completely masked until the fight is over. Even moderate to serious injuries like sprains, fractures and lacerations are much less obvious in the heat of combat.

Often the shock of being hit is more painful mentally than physically. When you get hit the first few times, you feel angry and frightened. Make a conscious effort to shake off this feeling and stick to your plan of attack. Don't become distracted by your fear or anger. Rather, focus on the event.

Accept the fact that in every combat situation, both fighters will be hit and sustain some physical damage. No matter how skilled you are, you cannot avoid being hit when you engage in one-on-one combat. Fighting is an exchange of blows. The person who sustains the least amount of damage prevails.

Another common fear is **fear of failure** or fear of losing. This is more of an illusory fear than the fear of injury. Being seriously injured is a reality that could change the course of your life forever. Losing or failing, is only a temporary emotional setback. If you have a great fear of failure, look at the possible root causes. Have you trained enough? Is your opponent much better than you? Do you have something to prove by fighting?

There are many causes of failing, ranging from poor training to just plain bad luck. Some you can control and some you cannot. Forget the uncontrollable. Look closely at the controllable factors like your determination to succeed, the amount and quality of your training, your ability and skill level. Assess each of these realistically. If you find that something is truly lacking, take action immediately to fix it.

More likely, you have become the victim of self doubt. Your skill does not change when you leave the training area and step into the combat site. But your self-perception might change. Try to focus on the reality of your present situation, rather than imagining all of the horrible things that could possibly happen.

If you cannot focus on success, think about the worst possible outcome. Is failing or losing really so awful? And even if it is, does it deserve your valuable time and emotion? Isn't there something more important for you to be thinking about at this critical time in your life?

NERVOUSNESS

Human beings are equipped with a special alert system that prepares them for new and dangerous adventures. Whether you are preparing to make a speech, run a race or fight for your life, your body goes through the same series of preparations. Called the "fight or flight" response, the brain signals the body to go on high alert.

All these reactions take place within minutes or even seconds of the perceived stimulus and may last for long periods of time.

In fact, an immediate threat is not always necessary to bring on this reaction. Anticipatory emotions such as anger, fear, anxiety and impatience can trigger the same response. When this happens, you feel "nervous". If you sense a threat and launch into immediate action, you do not feel nervous because your body is actively using the physical reactions and chemicals to respond. However, when you create an emotional build-up that causes the fight or flight response to occur without an immediate outlet, you feel the resulting physical response as digestive irritation, muscle tension, high blood pressure, irregular heart beat, hyperventilation, hyperactivity and other symptoms lumped together as nervousness.

The best cure for nervousness, then, is action. Give the body some activity to burn off the excess by-products of the response that is occurring. If you are about to engage in combat, do not attempt to remove the nervous feeling. A certain level of activation is desirable for combat. Try to maintain your activation level at two thirds of that which you will require in combat.

Recognize the nervousness for what it is - a physical preparation for upcoming activity. Practice controlling your arousal level so that it peaks just as you enter the peak activity stage. Arousal can be controlled in many ways. Some people are able to control it through psychological means such as visualization, self-talk, meditation, etc. For others, physical activity, like running, bouncing, stretching, or deep breathing works well.

Psychological controls are more likely to work before the response is beginning to take its course. Once the body begins releasing arousal chemicals, a certain amount of physical movement or the passage of time will be necessary to burn them off. In either case, know your body and your optimal arousal levels both before and during combat.

"Fight or Flight Reaction"

Response	Function
1. Adrenaline/noradrenaline are released directly into the blood stream	Sudden energy surge
2. Heart rate is increased Blood pressure rises Blood vessels dilate	Increase blood flow to facilitate delivery of necessary oxygen/ chemicals
3. Digestive process is shut down and blood is diverted to core systems from the stomach and skin	Allows increased circulation
4. Sweating increases	Cools the body
5. Liver converts glycogen into blood sugar	Instant energy surge
6. Breathing becomes shallower	Increased oxygen intake and waste removal
7. Muscle tension increase	Prepares muscles for high output activity

ANGER

Fear and nervousness are both natural and positive safety reactions to combat. Anger, however, is not. Anger is not rooted in the primal need for self-protection. It is an emotion of conflict and the inability to deal with a given conflict. Very few skilled fighters use anger to prepare for a fight.

Although anger is often the impetus for a real life confrontation, it has to be dispelled as the first blows are exchanged if you want to succeed. Anger destroys your emotional balance and prevents clear thought and judgment. It leads to an uncontrollable level of arousal.

If you feel angry with your opponent, channel that feeling into a more positive desire to win or to succeed through your plan.

If the anger is rooted in something other than the combat situation, try to remove it, or at least control it, before you engage the opponent.

YOUR OPPONENT'S EMOTION

Your opponent will be feeling many of the same emotions you are. This is often difficult to imagine, but it is true. If your opponent looks cool and focused, it is not because he is not scared and nervous, but because he has learned to control his emotions and understands his optimal arousal level.

To take advantage of your opponent's emotional state, consider how to intensify his fear. Look for ways to destroy his controlled psychological state. Many fighters try to scare their opponents by appearing menacing, vicious or tough.

When the conflict begins, attack to the most painful and sensitive targets. Demoralize him by increasing his fear of injury and pain. Take every physical and psychological advantage to defeat him. Refuse to be affected by his outward appearance or scare tactics. Look straight at him with a calm, confident stare and never give him the edge.

CHAPTER 4
ANALYSIS OF COMBAT SITUATIONS

"Know the enemy and know yourself; in a hundred battles you will never be in peril. When you are ignorant of the enemy but know yourself, your chances of winning or losing are equal. If ignorant of both your enemy and yourself, you are certain in every battle to be in peril."
-Sun Tzu

Knowing the enemy comes from experience and instinct. Often the enemy is unknown until the moment of engagement. He conceals his strengths and weaknesses as you do. He watches and waits and studies. He is not prepared to reveal even the smallest clue to his vulnerability. How, then, can you know him well enough to defeat him?

Knowing the enemy begins with knowing the type of tactician he is. By assessing his physical characteristics and his style of movement, we can draw certain general conclusions about his type.

If the opponent hides his level of skill, his mental condition or his weaknesses well, draw him out by feinting a very strong attack. Make him think you intend to finish the fight immediately. His gut reaction will be to defend himself fully. In this instant, you will see exactly what he is.

Qualities of Opponent Assessment

1. Size	4. Endurance
2. Strength	5. Weakness
3. Skill	6. Mental Conditioning

The following is a more detailed analysis of some characteristics through which you can categorize opponents.

HEIGHT

TALLER OPPONENT

A taller opponent will try to use his reach advantage to prevent you from coming within striking range of any of his targets. He will hit you or cut your movement whenever you try to penetrate his safety zone. To counteract his strategy, stay out of his range until you are prepared to attack. Once you decide to attack, use quick footwork to dart in, attack, destroy your target and retreat quickly. This is called a guerrilla attack, in which a smaller, weaker body defeats a larger body by attacking quickly and covertly to the nerve center of the larger force.

Another strategy is to draw the opponent into attacking by outwaiting him. Simply wait until he becomes impatient and attacks. When he does, take advantage of your smaller body size by beating him to the attack. If two people begin moving simultaneously, the quicker one will be the victor. Rely on your size to make quick, compact movements.

The last method is to make him move by feinting. As soon as he takes the bait, make your move. While his striking weapon is in the air, attack with power and conviction to unbalance him.

Key points against taller opponent:

1. Guerrilla attack
2. Wait and simultaneous attack or counter
3. Feint and attack

SHORTER OPPONENT

Tall fighters always appear to have the physical advantage because of their reach. If you use your reach properly, by pushing the opponent away before he is able to penetrate your safety zone, you will be victorious against a smaller opponent. Be cautious, however, not to be trapped by a small, quick opponent. If he tries a hit-and-run strategy, don't retreat. Wait for him to come into range and grab him tightly. Use your size advantage to take him down or strike/kick before he can escape.

Key points against shorter opponent:

1. Maintain safety zone
2. Use size advantage in close fighting

STRENGTH/SPEED

STRONGER OPPONENT

By nature, an opponent will rarely be both extremely strong or extremely quick. Assess which characteristic is predominant in your opponent. If he relies primarily on his strength, counter him with speed and smarts. Avoid his full power attacks by evasion, deflection and intelligence. Frustrate his attack by striking in sudden unexpected ways to soft, weak targets like the eyes, groin, or throat. Make him doubt the effectiveness of his power by avoiding his blows and hurting him with quick, sharp strikes. When he is surprised or confused, use your best attack and commit to finishing the fight immediately.

Key points against a stronger opponent:

1. Use speed and smarts to avoid power blows
2. Frustrate with sharp, surprise attacks

QUICKER OPPONENT

A quick opponent often relies on his speed to make up for his lack of size or power. If he lacks power, engage in an exchange and absorb some of his blows. Show him that it will take more than speed to defeat you. When he comes in, grab him and overpower him with a lock, throw or takedown. Use your superior strength to immobilize his speed and win on the ground.

> **Key points against a quicker opponent:**
>
> 1. Retaliate with power blows inside
> 2. Immobilize speed

HAND/FOOT DOMINANT

HAND DOMINANT OPPONENT

Many fighters, especially those trained in western style fighting are heavily dependent on their hands for attack and defense. To break their defensive posture, attack to low section targets like the groin, knees, thigh, shin and ankle. Frustrate them with their inability to block low section attacks. Once you have established a pattern of lower body attacks, move up and work the upper body. Mix up your attacks to confuse and disenchant the opponent. Finally try to remove his lower body mobility to reduce the effectiveness of his hand attacks. Make him like a caged tiger, unable to attack what he cannot reach.

> **KEY POINTS AGAINST HAND DOMINANT FIGHTERS:**
>
> 1. Attack to low section
> 2. Remove lower body mobility

FOOT DOMINANT OPPONENT

A kicker relies on his ability to balance on one leg while attacking with the other. Your first strategy should be to attack his base leg whenever he kicks. Make him insecure in kicking, especially kicks that expose his base leg for a long period of time. When you get a good shot at his base leg, take him down with a sweep or throw. Once he is on the ground, his kicking ability will be virtually useless.

If you cannot get his base leg, attack to the high section to disrupt his visibility and prevent him from finding good kicking opportunities. Make him occupy his legs for balance and resistance in grappling and clinching. Don't give him the distance to succeed with his kicks. Stay away or cut-in and take him down. But take caution in close distance not to be hit by low kicks to exposed areas.

> **Key points against foot dominant opponents:**
>
> 1. Attack the base leg
> 2. Take to ground fighting

DISTANCE

DISTANCE FIGHTER

Distance fighters like to control the tone of the fight by dictating the distance at which they will confront you. For this type of fighter, patience is the key. The more you attempt to go against his strategy, the more frustrated you will become and the more times you will get hit. Instead of trying to change the distance, wait until he moves. Once he decides to move in for an attack, grab him and don't let go. Try a takedown or lock or just keep attacking without letting him regain his favored distance.

> **Key points against a distance fighter:**
>
> 1. Wait for him to move
> 2. Engage in grappling, stay close

CLOSE FIGHTER

Close fighters like to engage you and never let go. They are usually strong and able to take alot of punishment without giving in. Try to prevent them from engaging you physically. Keep your distance through long range attacks (kicking) and footwork (back and side steps). If you get trapped or taken down, attack immediately to the most vulnerable areas. Use unexpected attacks that are not common in grappling fights like stomach throws and rear hook takedowns. Try anything that a conventional grappler would not anticipate. Avoid playing by his rules.

> **Key points against a close fighter:**
>
> 1. Maintain a safe distance
> 2. Stick to unconventional moves in close

Beyond your general assessment of your opponent's abilities, rely on your instinct and natural responses to carry you through.

Keep in mind that these tactics work for everyone. If you see yourself in any one of these styles, analyze how an opponent may try to defeat you. Practice fighting against someone who knows these strategies. When you know how to defeat yourself, you can pursue your personal style more confidently.

GROUP PSYCHOLOGY

There is a special opponent that has to be considered by anyone who trains for self-protection - the group attack. By seeing the group as a single enemy, you can use the psychology of group dynamics to formulate your strategy. Every group depends on team morale and fighting spirit. If you are alone or outnumbered against two or more opponents, you have to demoralize the group before you can defeat it.

A group's weakness is the individuals who comprise it because they depend on the power of superior size. If one element of the group gives up the fight, the other elements begin to question their involvement as well. Often the group fights for the ideals of the group, more than for personal gain. Therefore, when the personal sacrifice outweighs the attachment to the group ideals, the group fragments.

Another weakness of groups is that they are often made up of a series of weak elements that have banded together for strength. They do not work well alone or when divided. They are basically weak, but derive their strength from the security of a strong leader and the buffer of being surrounded by others.

The quickest way to demoralize a group is to attack the leader. When the leader is defeated, the group will fragment into smaller groups that will often begin to fight among themselves. Once the group is fragmented, you have a greater chance of escaping.

You also must try to find the antagonizer. In every group there is at least one person who wants to take the position of the leader and will split from the group at the slightest chance of taking the power. Use this person as an ally in your fight to defeat the leader and fragment the group.

In group fighting, the only reasonable objective is to escape at your earliest opportunity with the least amount of sustained damage possible. If you attempt to defeat the group for the sake of humiliating or revenging them, they will quickly coalesce against you. Don't give them any new motives to fight once you have made an opening for escape.

TERRAIN PSYCHOLOGY

By knowing how to take advantage of the environment, you gain an additional weapon. There are three types of terrain:

OPEN SPACE

Open spaces favor fighters who have good mobility and long weapons, whether bodily or environmental. They are a deterrent to fighters who like to fight in close because there is less chance to tie up and confine the opponent.

If you find yourself in an open space, aim for escape. If escape is not possible, keep your distance and avoid the opponent. Open spaces are the most favorable for fighting and have the highest possibility for escape without a great deal of damage.

CONFINED SPACE

Confined areas can be indoors or outdoors, including in vehicles. They can be confined on all sides or only a few. The primary characteristic of a confined space is that it limits the movements of the fighters. Confined spaces favor close fighters and grapplers. They require strength and endurance as well as creativity.

Confined spaces are ideal for defeating mobile, hit and run fighters. In a confined space, try to keep your opponent's back to the most confining barrier such as a wall. Keep you back to an opening. Avoid being pinned against any surface. Use the barriers around you to inflict damage to your opponent by driving him into them.

INCLINED SPACE

Inclined spaces can be either confined such as a stairwell or open such as a hillside. In either case, the strategy is the same, always try for the higher ground. Make the opponent attack upward and retreat downward. His attacks will be slow and require more strength. His retreating will be treacherous and always at risk of tumbling backwards down the incline.

By taking the higher ground, you open up his upper targets to attack more easily and your back is protected from a steep fall. You also have a better view of the surrounding area from your high perch.

If you cannot gain the highest position, try to topple the opponent by attacking to vital points of the lower body.

In any type of terrain, aim for the most advantageous position. If your opponent gains the better position, do not fight him for it. Instead, lead him away from it and when he strays far enough, double back and take the position you want. If you are not in a position to retreat, like in a confined space, try to convert both of your positions into neutral positions. Rather than having your back against the wall and your opponent pinning you, slip out so that both of you have one side against the wall. From this position you can further struggle to get the advantage.

When you get your opponent into any unfavorable position, do not allow him time to look around and assess his location. Distract and confuse him. Make him stumble and fall on uneven ground. Make him run into obstacles and become confined. Keep him constantly on the defensive.

BOOK   FIVE

THE WAY   OF   THE
WARRIOR

THE MAP

By practicing junsado, you learn to execute the techniques and strategies of combat. But, through combat experience, you realize that these tactics and strategies and techniques do not exist. They are just an abstract map.

Like a map of the Earth, the map is just a copy or drawing of what exists. The Earth exists without the map. It is a separate entity. The map is the guide to help us navigate the parts of the Earth that cannot readily be seen with our eyes. With our sight, we can see only a short distance, so the map allows us to expand our concept of the Earth and plan trips to places where we have never been. It enables us to expand our world beyond that which we can readily see.

If the Earth changes, we must change our map to accommodate the changes. If a volcano erupts and destroys a city, we must remove it from the map. We cannot insist on going to the city simply because it still exists on our map. Keeping the map up to date allows us to save time and energy.

But if we change the map, it does not change the shape or size of the Earth. Simply crossing a city off the map does not make it disappear. The Earth is a constant existence beyond our individual control. We can only seek to understand it and live harmoniously with it, not control it.

Combat is the same. The combat itself is not directly under our control. We can use our strategies and techniques to navigate safely through combat, even that which we have never experienced. But we cannot change the entire combat simply by changing the techniques and strategies we practice. Combat often exists independently of us. To survive, we must sense the changes of combat and adjust to them using our strategic map.

Because you prepare a wide variety of excellent throwing skills does not mean the combat will change so you can use them. The combat exists as it is. If it is the type of combat in which throwing works well, you will succeed. If it is the type of combat that requires striking or locking or weapons skills, you will fail. You will become the victim of your plan.

Do not be attached to the map. See the reality of combat and adjust your map accordingly. Do not allow combat to change without you. Search for truth in your training and truth in combat. There is only one truth. All else is just the illusion of the map.

DUALITY

When you remove the concept of winning, the concept of losing will disappear. Think about it. What is a loser without a winner or a winner without a loser? One cannot exist without the other. They exist for the sake of each other.

When you remove winning and losing, you remove the fear of combat. Without winning and losing, there is only doing. Doing takes place until the task is completed. Finish and move on. Fear comes from the illusion that there is an outcome of every combat. But in reality, there is not. There is only the action and interaction of two or more people. They contest every instant, every movement.

Then what is the actual outcome? Today you fight a weaker opponent and win. Tomorrow you fight a stronger opponent and lose. What is the reality of the outcome? It is merely a relative judgment of the skills of two people at specific moment in time and space. The moment passes, the opponent changes and the outcome is different. There are no absolute winners or losers. There are only abstract comparisons.

Until you remove the duality of winning and losing, you cannot master combat. Mastery of combat comes from being part of the process of struggling without regard for anything other than the present moment. The ultimate warrior finishes the fight and looks back not once. He looks only forward.

He can do this because he fought with his total skill and concentration. He has nothing to regret or boast of because he did his humble best knowing it is the best he has to give. Yet he knows that combat is ever changing and every battle holds new challenge. There is never time to proclaim absolute victory or defeat.

When the duality of thought is gone, the human spirit is free to be as it is. There is no comparison or judgment or self. There is only the desire to soar higher and higher with every thought and action.

SIGHT AND PERCEPTION

Humans have two distinct ways of understanding the world around them - sight and perception. Sight is the most common and obvious. Perception is more abstract and functions at a higher level.

In combat, sight is essential for success. Without sight, the average combatant would easily be struck down in seconds. Sight allows us to process large amounts of sensory information in fractions of a second. It is our first line of defense against any frontal attack.

However, sight is useful only for processing information that is in a state of existence. We can see an opponent attempting to kick or punch us. We can see a car about to run us over. We can see a dog preparing to attack. The physical actions in these cases are readily evident.

But the intent of the movements is what is most important in preparing a reaction. How can we know if the opponent has raised his hand to punch us or to give a high five? How do we know whether the car is simply driving up to meet us or really intends to run us down? How can we tell whether the dog is playful or vicious?

These judgments stem from perception. Perception is the assessment of the intangible characteristics of a situation. In these given situations, the intangibles are obvious. We can assess the demeanor and prior actions of the assailant, the speed at which the car is traveling, the expression and nature of the dog. Here our perception will be accurate and keep us safe.

When there are many visible characteristics of a scene, we can combine sight and perception and make an accurate judgment. When the visual contents are vague, abstract or deceptive, sight can be untrustworthy. Human intellect provides many tools of deception. A potential assailant may appear harmless, but there is a certain feeling of uneasiness that you feel in his company.

Therefor, when in doubt rely on perception. Every skilled warrior has been saved many times by perception alone. It is a feeling that he cannot explain to anyone, but one that proves to be true when the outcome is revealed. Cultivate your understanding of the unseen as well as the seen. By knowing what exists in front of your eyes, you can know that which is invisible as well.

ACTION

Human action is the expression of human thought. Every action is preceded by a thought in which the action is formulated. Whether the thought is conscious, as in ''I think I'll go for a walk'' or unconscious as in breathing, the brain controls the body. Without the brain, the body is dead.

Conscious thought is contrived by a rational thought process that can be altered to suit our character. Unconscious thought or brain processes are purely natural reactions to the needs and wants of our body. We need oxygen, so we breathe. Our organs require nutrients and waste removal so our heart circulates blood throughout the body. We rarely have to give conscious thought to breathing and is virtually impossible to consciously make our heart beat or not beat simply by thinking.

Our body demands and responds to those demands in perfect harmony. This is the ultimate goal of combat. Sense the demand of the situation and respond to it in perfect harmony. Bypass the conscious thought process and move in perfect synchronization with the flow of the combat.

The skills of combat exist for the combat itself, not for us. The skills fulfill the needs of combat situations. When we use the skills, we become the tool through which the skills are expressed. We are simply the catalyst for the actions.

A master of combat is one who knows that the actions of combat happen of him, not by him. He is the instrument of the action, not the perpetrator. When you allow the skills and tactics to flow freely, without interference from your conscious thought, you will cease to exist. Only the action exists. You and the action are the same.

OPENNESS

When there is openness, there is innovation. Open minds and open hearts lead the way in any society. Regardless of your level of skill or education, there is always a newer, better vision to seek out. You may not discover something on the scale of the world being round or the planets rotating around the sun, but human history and knowledge are the sum of human thought and discovery.

Innovation comes from those who are informed and willing to challenge that information. Junsado is based on human innovation. It is a living art. It is based on the knowledge of great strategists and the innovation of the human spirit based on this fundamental knowledge.

It is based on action, not theory. It is active and free in combat. It adapts to the change of combat without being attached to the map. It transcends the duality of comparison and judgment. It seeks to blend in with the natural laws of the universe. It pushes the practitioner ever higher in search of the still undiscovered perfect strategy.

UNITY

You are but one infinitesimal part of the universe. In the whole concept of space and time, your existence is almost nonexistent. Time and space exist with or without you. Your lifetime is limited to a span of time and when you cease to exist, the world will go on without you. Perhaps your passing will be marked by great ripples across the Earth, but more likely, it will be duly noted and life will go on without great disruption.

Then what is the purpose of your meager existence? To become greatness. You are limited only by the limits you place on yourself. If you see yourself as small and insignificant, you will be so. Instead, see yourself as part of a great and wondrous being. You are one part of the entire universe. You are not separate from it. You are part of the great continuum of time and space.

Aim at the totality of the human existence. Search for the new ground. Take yourself to the limits of your being and feel the power of the progression of time. Time will go on with or without you. Jump into the progress to the future with both feet.

Transcend the limitations of the mind. Human knowledge is fragmented and partial. There is much left to be created and discovered, but only by those who can break out of the concept of being a small part of the universe into the concept of being an integral part of the universe.

GLOSSARY

Action timing - the tempo required for successfully striking the opponent with an initiative attack

Assimilation - the process of taking in or incorporating into one's own body

Circular attack - a skill or technique that strikes its target by moving on an arced course

Closed Stance (CS) - a stance where, when the opponents face each other, both have the same foot (i.e. right) forward

Combat - a fight or conflict between two or more parties

Combination - a series of offensive and defensive maneuvers linked together by some unifying themes or factors

Combined response - the actions of the primary and secondary responses

Conventional tactics - those combat skills which are ordinarily accepted as standard for achieving victory

Counterattack - a skill executed so as to penetrate the opponent's defenses by exploiting a weakness created by the opponent's attack

Direct attack - a skill or technique that strikes the opponent without requiring prior action on the part of either combatant

Draw - a form of indirect attacking by which the opponent is shown a weakness or opening to lure him into a vulnerable position

Feint - a form of indirect attack by which the opponent is deceived into committing his defenses to a simulated attack thereby leaving himself vulnerable

Fight or flight response - the physiological and psychological reactions that take place in the human body when it is placed under stress or duress

Full stance - conservative defensive stance characterized by alignment of the feet, concealment of the center line and agility of sideways movement

Half Stance - aggressive offensive stance characterized by a stable base, forward facing trunk and powerful forward movement

Indirect attack - a skill or technique that strikes the opponent by first creating another movement on the part of one or both combatants

Junsado - the art of strategy and tactics in which adaptation and effectiveness are the primary strengths

Lateral - of or pertaining to the side (as an attack to the side of the body)

Left Stance (LS) - any stance in which the right foot is forward

Linear attack - a skill or technique that strikes its target by moving on a straight course

Open Stance (OS) - a stance where, when both opponents face each other, one has the right foot forward the other has the left foot forward

Planar - of or pertaining to a flat or level surface

Primary Response - the segment of combat in which the opponent's attack is neutralized and the secondary response prepared

Reaction timing - the tempo required for successfully striking the opponent with an indirect attack

Right Stance (RS) - any stance in which the left foot is forward

Secondary Response - the segment of combat in which the confrontation is decisively ended

Set-up - a form of indirect attack that exploits the habits or thinking patterns of the opponent

Strategy - a plan or method for maximum utilization of power through long range planning and development to obtain a specific goal such as to ensure victory or security

Tactics - deployment of the physical skills necessary to execute strategy

Triangle force frame - an offensive or defensive foundation where the practitioner forms a triangle with his body by setting up a strong base for stability and a strong apex for attacking or defending

Unconventional tactics - those combat skills which are not ordinarily accepted as standard elements necessary for achieving success in combat.

ABOUT THE AUTHOR

Hanho, with over 30 years experience in the martial arts, holds Master rankings in taekwondo, hapkido, kendo and junsado. In addition to his extensive training background, he has obtained first hand combat knowledge through his service as a counter espionage agent in the South Korean Defense Security Command, an elite branch of the special forces. During his service, he was also a hand-to-hand combat and survival instructor for the Korean Special Forces and the Eight Command of the United States Army stationed in Korea.

ABOUT JUNSADO

For more information about the junsado system of strategy and tactics or the Junsado Combat Strategy Video Series write:

JUNSADO
c/o Turtle Press
P.O. Box 290206
Wethersfield, CT 06129-0206

Index